Energy Healing for Horses

A Comprehensive Guide to Learning

Holly Davis

Copyright © 2014 Holly Davis

All Rights Reserved.

This book may not be reproduced in whole or part in any form or by any means, electronic, mechanical, or otherwise without permission from the Author. Except by a reviewer, who may quote brief paragraphs in a review.

For all other permissions, please contact the Author

www.hollydavis.co.uk

ISBN-10:1505578345
ISBN-13:978-1505578348

DEDICATION

A massive 'Thank you' to all the horses that have made my life, what it is today, to my friends and family for their support. Also to all my various teachers, be they two or four legged, who have enabled me to learn from them and have shared their time with me. Without all of you, this book would not have been in print today.

To the horses….
I am sorry that so many people do not listen to you….
That so many ignore your cries….
But I am trying to help you to be heard, each and everyday.

**"We must educate our children to enable love and compassion for all living things.
By doing this we can create a peaceful future for all."**

ACKNOWLEDGMENTS

Book Cover

Samantha Mignano at Beyond Metrix

Photograph by Elenore Bowden-Bird

Aulanda Park Equine Liberty

Susan and Tim Duckworth at Bitless and Barefoot

All of the kind people that have so kindly given their permission for me to share photographs of their beautiful horses, with you.

Kayleigh, Hope, Meeka, Polly, Texas, Cinders, Smithy McCord, Alfi, Manta, Harree and all the other beautiful horses that have shared their wisdom with me.

CONTENT

What is Equine Energy Therapy?.....Page 12
Why give healing to horses?
How does it work?
What equine energy therapy is not
Where does the healing energy come from?
Distance healing
All thought is energy
Life force energy
Grounding
Vertical axis alignment
Using a Healer for your horse
UK Veterinary Law
The permission issue

The Horse's Energy Systems.....Page 22
Auric layers
Chakras
Meridians

Body Scanning.....Page 28
Body Scanning in person
Scanning tack and other equipment

How to Give a Healing Session.....Page 30
Energy transference
Common equine reactions during a healing session
The Theta state
Grounding
Protection

Mental Energy Tools.....Page 35
The energy tap
The sea of emotion
The chakra fan
The sewing kit
Energy putty

Energy blockages
Colours and numbers
Energy cords
Chakra balancing
Trauma blasts
Water vibration
Reading the horses aura

Natural Healing and Other Therapies…..Page 45
Crystal healing
Essential oils
Chiropractic
Homeopathy
Herbs
Spiritual healing
Radionics
Colour therapy

The Human and Horse Link…..Page 51
The owner and riders influence
The horse's emotions
When a horse is very ill or dies
Support of the owner
Integrity and mental focus
Munchausen by Proxy

Types of Aggression…..Page 61
Stallions
The Alfa Mare
The True Leader
The Enforcer
Early weaning

The Horse as a Prey Animal…..Page 68
Self harming
Holistic Horse Management
The barefoot horse
Rehabilitation
The horse's eyesight

Seasonal affective disorder

The Horse's Soul.....Page 74

Horse Vices.....Page 75
Endorphins
Natural horsemanship
Nutritional requirements
Toxins

The Equine Star Chakras.....Page 79
Healing through the bladder meridian
Etheric light crystals
Epilepsy in horses
The horses past lives
The horse's present past life
The horse's life path
Past life injury and trauma
The horse's blueprint
The original trauma line
Lost soul parts
The golden energy hoop

Basics of Dowsing.....Page 92
Types of dowsing tools
How does dowsing work?
Using a pendulum
Typical pendulum responses
Directional dowsing
Refining your newly found skill
Advanced pendulum responses
Clear your mind and connect
Working with non attachment and appropriate timing
Blind dowsing

Earth and Environmental Allergies.....Page 100

Grounding the Horse to the Earth.....Page 101
Connecting the horse to home

Divinity in horses
Working with the second heart chakra

Metal Shoes and Bits…..Page 104
Bitless bridles
The centaur experience
The Horse as a guide
Negative emotions
The organs and their associated emotions

The Horse as a Guide…..Page 109
The horse as a guide
Sympathy vs Empathy
Negative emotions
The organs and their associated emotions

Bach Flower Remedies
Rescue Remedy

Resources………….Page 119

About the Author….Page 123

What is Equine Energy Therapy?

Energy Healing aims to help restore and rebalance the bodies own naturally existing energies. These energies are well documented in Traditional Chinese Medicine (TCM) and are known as:

Jing - A lower physical energy found in the body including the blood.

Chi -.An overall energy that flows through the Aura, Chakras and Meridian Systems and throughout the whole of the physical body.

Shen - The higher spiritual energy.

There are many ways in which we can help these energies to come into balance. In this book we will be studying the practices of hands on healing, flower remedies and also looking at other widely available holistic therapies that are in common use with horses today.

Why Give Healing to Horses?

If we look back into the past at the history of the horse it is easy to see how their lives have changed and become much more stressful.

Some of us choose to stable our horses. This can be very foreign to them with regards to their natural instinct and way of life as a prey animal. It can give some horses the feeling of being trapped with nowhere to run to for safety. On top of this we often feed our horses on grains and other foods that are not best suited to their sensitive digestion systems. Many domesticated horses in the UK are also turned out the graze in lush green pasture best suited to cattle. Horses tend to benefit more on rough grazing due to the risk of laminitis. Owners and riders can also cause emotional upset and distress to horses. It could be that the person is neglectful, sharp or intolerant of their horse when they are misunderstanding their emotional needs or what is being asked of them. As well as stables, we also ask horses to travel in trailers and horse lorries that are far removed from anything their instincts tell them is natural. Is it then of any wonder that so many have issues with being loaded onto such vehicles?

On top of all this we ask them to carry us on their backs, which is not something that nature intended them to do. A bad or unbalanced rider may pull at their mouth or cause them to have to move in a way that over time causes them tension which when left unattended to will lead to physical pain. So is it fair to say that many horses lead quite a difficult life?

There is a lot of truth in the saying 'I love my horse to death', as people quite often literally do. By spoiling a horse and not teaching them calmly and firmly about boundaries we can cause all kinds of stress and confusion issues for the horse. Of course, another way we can 'love them to death' is by over rugging them, over feeding them or quite literally making their life a general misery.

How does it Work?

The horse's energy systems are made up of vibrational frequencies, each with their own unique patterning. When a horse becomes ill and suffers trauma these frequencies can become distorted. When left like this over a long period of time the distorted frequencies can cause disruption within the physical body. This is because the energy systems act as a blueprint or foundation for the physical body and good health. The aim of energy healing is to help to rebalance these frequencies in the correct way the individual needs so that we can give them the best chance at regaining their physical and emotional health. Understanding that it works this way also enables us to see why healing is of benefit to horses that also appear, to be emotional and physically well as healing can also act as a prevention. By correcting these energetic disruptions early on it may even be the case that some emotional and physical illness can be avoided before they manifest.

Healing isn't hard to do if the love, desire and integrity needed exists within that person, this alone is what makes it work best.

What Equine Energy Therapy is not

Firstly and most importantly energy therapy is not a replacement for veterinary care. Veterinary permission should always be sought before any laying on of hands is done by anyone other than the horse's guardian. If you are not in the UK it may also be wise to check the relevant laws for your country with regards to treating someone else's horse. Equine Energy Therapy is considered to be a complementary therapy, the term 'alternative therapy' can give rise to misinterpretation if it is used instead of professional medical care, rather than along side it.

Whilst it is possible that this therapy can and has worked what may seem like miracles at is important not to become purest about it and believe that it is the only true way to heal a horse, to do so could be putting their lives in danger. It is important to understand that in many cases it does have it's limitations, that part will be down to the horse itself by only taking what it needs and only when it is ready to accept it.

Where does the Healing Energy come from?

The energies that we use are omnipresent meaning that they are in everything and are everywhere throughout the universe. By directing our healing we can harness these energies and use them, channeling them into the direction where they are most needed. Science has shown that although energy can change it cannot cease to exist which is good to hear as this means we will never run out!

Distance Healing

Distance healing works in much the same way as hands on healing although obviously the horse isn't physically present. You may like to visualise the horse in your mind, or just thinking of them maybe enough for you to maintain your focus. Concentrate your intent towards this individual horse (or maybe even a whole herd of horses) it must always for their highest good and in their best interests.

At this point you may feel the energies leaving your hands or may even just feel an all over body physical sensation, everyone is different. You may feel nothing physically at all but instead you maybe left with a sense of knowing that the healing has been sent and completed. Once the healing session has come to an end, give thanks to the energies that have worked with you.

All Thought is Energy

Now that we are ready to start to understand how we can help to heal horses we need to understand some of the other energetic dynamics behind it.

Every thought that comes to mind, every word we speak and every single intention that we have carries a vibrational signature. When intention is put behind a word whilst even thinking of it, or thinking about the horse it can have a positive or negative effect on them depending on the type of word it is. The words we send out and receive when thinking aren't so much what the animal receives from us as the energetic dynamic behind the spoken word and what it means and represents to them. We can understand this by accessing how we feel when people speak to us; not only by the words they use but also by how those words make us feel when used with intent and emotion behind them.

Example

If someone tells us that they hate us it will cause us a very different feeling to when someone tells us that they love us. Just as the word 'danger' carries a very different vibration and feeling to the word 'safe'. When we are with a horse or even away from them for that matter, in order to help the animal feel as comfortable as possible we need to phase our thoughts and words in a positive way.

Example

'Nothing will hurt you in your stable. No one will ever hit you again when you are in there'.

The above statement when received energetically in a fragmented manner by the horse can bring about negativity due to these parts: 'hurt you' and 'hit you'.

We can change the feeling or mental statement to: 'you will always be safe in your stable and will always feel comfortable with people in there.' This will give the statement an overall positive feeling.

In the same way negativity can have a bigger impact on some horses than others. For some horses emotional discord is far more distressing than physical disharmony and vice versa. What one horse might call a 'smack' another horse might see as a 'beating'. In the same way if two horses have a food bowl thrown at them by their owner in temper each might view it in a very different way due to the intent behind it. One may view it as distressing and see the frustration behind it and feel scared, whilst another may feel their human's emotions and know that they aren't angry with them, they are frustrated and upset about something else so the horse knows that this display is not aimed at them personally. The outcome due to feeling the emotion and intent behind the throwing of the food bowl at them can bring about a different feeling with regards to the situation and therefore, a totally different outcome as to how they feel about it and view it.

The moment we choose or intend to connect with any horse they know how we are feeling at that time and this will have an influence on our energy and the way in which the horse interprets it. If we are feeling under the weather, negative, angry or in any other way not positive, if we are not feeling as comfortable to connect as we should the horse might not be so willing to work with us or be around us.

By assessing our own feelings and dispelling with any negative thoughts we are holding onto we make ourselves much more approachable and comfortable to be around.

We also need to assess our intention and our integrity. What is our intention? Are we purely in this job for the money? Or is it because if we can find out about the horse's physical illness we might be able to save our self from an expensive veterinary diagnosis and treatment? Is it that we want to impress people? Or is it because we genuinely have a heartfelt desire to help?

Whatever the intention behind your communication the horse will know the moment that you connect with them. If your intentions aren't of the highest integrity, the healing can be affected.

When we choose to communicate for the wrong reasons it may well be that whilst the horse is happy to let us work with them, aiding them with their day to day issues and about medical problems they may not feel comfortable enough to express deep emotional issues that could be the underlying problem behind all it's other problems in the first place, as the horse doesn't feel as safe with your energy as it should.

Life Force Energy

Chi energy is within all living things from trees and animals to people. There are many interpretations as to what this life force energy actually is. Some people believe it to the animal's consciousness, essence or true self, which all basically come down to the same thing. It is not uncommon for equine practitioners that have clairvoyant abilities (Clairvoyant – Clear seeing) to see a white butterfly leaving the horses body at the onset or, during it's physical passing. This is often seen as being symbolic of the horse's psyche or soul leaving it's now discarded and no longer needed body, or it's vehicle that enabled it to move through its physical life.

Some experiments have been carried out during the human death experience that have shown the physical body weighs slightly less after death than before death. There would appear to be no rational explanation for this. Could the leaving of the soul account for this, maybe?

However, what we do know is that soon after death the life force energy slowly leaves the physical body and that it is impossible for a horse to live and breathe without this energy. Often in the cases of horses that are terminally ill, or near passing through old age, these life force energy levels are found to be very low and slowly disappear up to or soon after physical death. Without it's life force energy the horse would not be able to live.

Grounding

Those that have previous experience of meditation and energy work will likely have knowledge of grounding exercises. The most commonly used exercise for grounding is through the visualisation of being a tree and growing roots and connecting into the earth. This is all very well but we all know what happens when the wind blows! The tree can be uprooted, sway and can become unstable. Because of this the best mediation for grounding that I have found so far is the vertical axis alignment exercise that I have been teaching for the past 15 years.

Grounding is very important in any kind of energy work as it enables us to hold our focus in the here and now and remain mentally and emotionally present.

Vertical Axis Alignment

In order to carry out this exercise you need to first stand up straight with your feet pointing forwards, shoulder width apart. Do not hold too much tension in your knees when doing this or remain too rigid, as your muscles and frame need to be relaxed.

Close your eyes and take a few deep breaths. Now imagine a vertical cord in the centre of your stomach. The cord stretches up through your spine and out through the top of your head. From here it connects to wherever it is you come from. You do not need to know where this is the intention is enough.

Now go back to your stomach area and locate the other end of the cord.

Now imagine this cord stretching down, splitting and going down each leg and into the ground, deeper and deeper and into the centre of the earth where it anchors.

Now imagine a conker on a piece of string. When the string is not tight the conker will wobble. But when we tighten the string at each end it will remain solid. In order to achieve stability we need to make sure our connections at each end of our cord are well anchored. Imagine the cord tightening, pulling both up and down and stabilising us.

Whilst this is going on we may feel different sensations, such as:

A wobbling or shaky feeling in our legs.

The sensation of being pulled up or down, or even both.

We may sway forwards and backwards.

Once the process is completed and we are fully grounded. We will feel nice and stable and are ready to allow the process to come to an end, take a deep breath and open your eyes. This exercise can be used at any time we feel we need to ground ourselves, not just within our energy work.

Using a Healer for Your Horse

If you intend to use a Healer for your horse it is best to find someone recommended. An ethical person will be suitably qualified and insured and will follow the correct regulations with regards to veterinary law.

UK Veterinary Law

With regards to treating an animal in person the law states:

Protection of Animals Act 1911

Legally the owner of any animal may give appropriate treatment so long as it is not considered physically invasive.

The Veterinary Surgeons (exemptions) Order of 1962

It is illegal for any complementary therapy to be administered to an animal by anyone other than the animal's owner unless veterinary permission is first granted.

Please Note Healing is not a replacement for veterinary care and attention. Anyone who allows an animal to suffer through withholding veterinary attention can be prosecuted.

It is illegal for anyone other than a Veterinary Surgeon to diagnose an animal. However you may pass on any information that the horse is giving you as this could be useful to the horse's Veterinary Surgeon, it may go along way in helping the Vet with a medical diagnosis. Even if you find yourself in the situation where the horse is telling you directly that it has a certain illness it is best advised that the symptoms it is feeling are passed on rather than attempting an actual diagnosis. Actual diagnosis is best left to the medical profession.

The Permission Issue

People tend to have different views about permission. With regards to healing permission is very important and healing should only be given with the intention of it being for the horse's highest good. The reason being that by healing a certain emotional problem or physical issue we may well be taking away the horses natural ability to deal with it or heal it themselves, in some cases it may impede their own learning and understanding.

You may come across situations where a person doesn't want you to do healing on their horse even though you may know that the horse is in desperate need.

In these circumstances it very much comes down to how you feel about the situation and what you are willing or not willing to do about it. Firstly we can question whether we need the owner's permission at all? As surely we do not need permission to send distance healing to another living being from someone else when the horse is obviously wanting to accept it and is in need. Surely the decision should be left entirely up to the horse? This however is a personal decision best left to the individuals that find themselves in this situation. An owner's refusal to allow you to give healing to their horse, maybe through their own fear of where the healing comes from. Whether or not you choose to send healing to the horse under these circumstances is very much a personal choice, but the free will of the horse should always be taken into consideration. It might just be that by sending healing to a horse that is in need of it not only are you helping them to rebalance their energies but you are also making them aware that someone (you) are willing to listen.

The Horse's Energy Systems

The horses energy systems are made up of three main energy bodies: The Chakras, the Aura and the Meridians. The collective name for these energy systems is the 'Etheric Body' as it consists purely of energy.

The Aura exists within and around physical body. It has many different layers the main ones being:

First Layer - Physical Plane
This relates to the base chakra. It bridges the connection between the energy body and the physical body.

Second Layer – Emotional Body
This relates to the sacral chakra. It is associated with the vibrations of inner feelings.

Third Layer – Mental Body
This relates to the solar plexus chakra. It is associated with the vibrations of the ego, mental thought processes and our thoughts.

Fourth Layer – Astral Body
This relates to the heart chakra. It is associated with our expressions

of feeling on a mental, emotional and physical level.

Fifth Layer – Spiritual Plane
This is related to the throat chakra. It is our blueprint for the lower etheric body.

Sixth Layer – Celestial Body
This relates to the brow chakra. It is associated with our 'enlightenment'.

Seventh Layer – (Ketheric) Casual Body
This relates to the crown chakra. It is associated with our connection to the divine.

Eighth Layer - Cosmic Plane
This is associated with to our past and future karma and is our link to the Akashic Records.

Ninth Layer – Soul Body
This is associated with the connection between where we are now and what we perceive as heaven.

Tenth Layer – Integrative Body
This is associated with the connection between the physical and spiritual worlds. It is able to disconnect from the physical body to enter into the astral realms.

It is not unusual to find as many as fourteen auric layers within the horse's aura, sometimes even more. Old disruptive emotions and trauma from past events can become stuck in the aura causing vibrational disturbance. It is not at all unusual to come across holes and other wounds in the aura. These can come about through trauma of being separated from or the death of a love one that has been either wrenched away (for example during weaning) or through a horse not being able to grieve over the death of a field companion or a still born foal. By helping to restore traumatized areas within this energy system not are we only able to help the horse emotionally but also physically.

This is also one of the most commonly affected energy systems as it is so wide spread that it is open to mixing with other energies as simply as a horse standing along side another horse, not to mention how closely the intermingling of the auras are with the riders when being ridden.

Chakras

Horses like people have major and minor charkas. The major charkas are those that are larger and run along the spinal column whilst the minor ones are situated throughout the body including the hooves, knees, hocks and the tips of the ears. They are often viewed as a vortex that spirals through the body and out of the opposite side or as a tunnel or a flat circular disc, depending on your own interpretation. The word Chakra comes from the Sanskrit word meaning circle or wheel.

Each chakra relates to certain areas of the body.

Base or Root Chakra
Location: Base of the spine
Colour: Red
Element : Earth
Sense: Smell
Associated with: Acceptance, stability, grounding and Survival

Sacral Chakra
Location: Pelvis
Colour: Orange
Element: Water
Sense: Taste
Associated with: Kidneys, adrenals, reproductive system .and lymphatic system

Solar Plexus Chakra
Location: Centre of the back
Colour: Yellow
Element: Fire
Sense: Sight
Associated with: Digestive system, liver and stomach.

Heart Chakra
Location: In between the shoulder blades and in the centre of the chest
Colour: Pink
Element: Air
Sense: Feel
Associated with: Thymus gland, heart and lungs.

Throat Chakra
Location: Throat area
Colour: Blue
Element: Heavens
Sense: Hearing
Associated with: Thyroid gland, throat and mouth

Brow or Third Eye Chakra
Location: Centre of the forehead
Colour: Indigo
Element: Silver
Associated with: Eyes, nose, ears, pituitary gland, skeletal system

The Second Heart Chakra

This is a chakra that I discovered some years ago whilst using with healing work on my Appaloosa horse. It is situated in the centre of the horses flank and forms a 'tunnel' through and out of the opposite flank. Though it is part of the horse's chakra system it is also separate from it in as much as this is the chakra that links them to the healing of others. This chakra will be found closed in many animals as they are yet emotionally unable to take on their healing role due to their own trauma. Once they are ready the chakra will open and they will take on the role as natural born healers. Most four legged animals have his chakra in their systems with the exception of sheep other than the odd individual one. Under no circumstances should this chakra be opened until the animal is ready as to do so could bring mental and emotional upset due to the added stress of sensitivity.

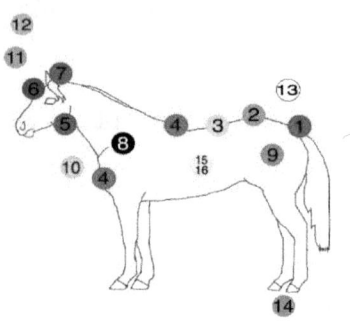

1. Base - B
2. Sacral - S
3. Solar Plexus - SP
4. Heart - H
5. Throat - T
6. Third Eye - TE
7. Crown - C
8. Brachial - B
9. Second Heart - SH
10. Thymus - TH
11. Soul Star - SS
12. Stellar Gateway - SG
13. Home Star - HS
14. Earth Star - ES
15/16. Balance Left/Right - BL/R

Meridians

These are energy pathways throughout the body some of which are linked to major organs. They are used in Chinese medicine for acupuncture and acupressure treatments. There are 66 meridians in all. Only 14 of these meridians are commonly known of and used. Different meridians in the body carry slightly different energy. We will focus on the most commonly used meridians that are known to carry 'Chi' throughout the body. Each meridian has a partner meridian that it works in conjunction with and has connections to.

Jing Creative and Generative Energy
Chi Life Force Energy
Shen Spiritual Energy

Wood Element Meridians
Liver and gall bladder
Colour: Green

Fire Element Meridians
Heart and small intestine
Colour: Red

Earth Element Meridians
Stomach and spleen
Colour: Orange

Metal Element Meridians
Lung and Large intestine
Colour: Grey

The Conception Vessel and the Governing Vessel
Length of the spine, front and back of the body
Colour: Black or white

The **Etheric Body** is the blue print for the physical. When parts of the energy system become blocked or disrupted the imbalances can filter through to the physical body leading to ill health. By maintaining them in a healthy balance we can aid physical, mental and emotional well-being.

Body Scanning

There are several ways that we can scan a horse. We can choose to scan them physically or mentally, in person or at distance, or choose to the scan the physical body or the energy systems.

Body Scanning in Person

When we are in the company of the horse that we are going to body scan we have several options. We can choose to hold our hands on the horse or just above the horse to see what physical sensations we pick up. These could include:

Tingling
A knowing of where to place our hands and for how long
Electric shock type feelings
Heat or cold
Just go with your intuition as to what needs to be done.

We can also choose to mentally scan the horse. Often closing our eyes helps us to focus as when we have our eyes open we can revert back to the wide awake beta brainwave state.

Alternatively we can move our eyesight around the horse's physical body, taking note of any areas that you are drawn to or see energy in that shouldn't be there. If you find this difficult relax a little more and don't try too hard.

We may prefer to close our eyes and visualize the horse in our mind. Move your line of sight all around the horse whilst looking for any areas that may be indicated to us. This may come in the form of colour or fog over certain areas of the body, dark areas, or just areas that our mind sight keeps being drawn to.

We can also try distance body scanning in much the same way. Some people may choose to visualize just the outline of a horse with the intention that this is a certain individual. Others may prefer to see a photograph of the horse and then close their eyes and picture them that way.

Scanning Tack and Other Equipment

When using our 'second sight' or 'minds eye' to view energy we are also able to scan other things, it may include the scanning of tack, bridles and bits. This enables us to check for correct fit and comfort. When one or more of these items cause discomfort or constriction to the horse they will also cause an energetic imbalance that is possible to see through energy sight. For the purpose of the remainder of this book I will use the term 'Energy Sight' to mean the mental or visual use of seeing energetic disruptions. We can use our energy sight by either looking for any trace energetic disruptions and residual energies left over from when the equipment was last used or by mentally fitting the piece of equipment and looking for any energetic imbalances. By mentally fitting a bridle or saddle in our minds onto a horse we can use our energy sight to mentally view any areas of dark coloured or foggy energy that can be found there. Often we may find that although a bit or saddle appears to fit it maybe that the animal has a large tongue that causes the bit to sit on a slant or that a saddle is symmetrical when the animal isn't. It is also not uncommon for there to be manufacturing faults deep within the saddle that can cause the horse problems when the weight of a rider is added, such as incorrect or lumpy stuffing or even a small piece of loose leather that has been left inside during manufacture.

How to Give a Healing Session

In order to give a healing session we must first make sure that we are properly 'grounded'. This is the term that I will use for making sure that we are fully here in the present and focused.

Once we are fully grounded we first need to stand with the horse for a few minutes giving them the chance to sniff us, maybe lick us and make sure that they are comfortable with us around them. Of course this will not always be the case, as chances are you will be asked to work with abused or traumatised horses that aren't comfortable with a stranger or even sometimes anyone near them. If this turns out to be the case then stand back from the animal and just observe them for a few minutes. This will enable them to get used to you being present and to give them the chance to understand that you are not there to over step their boundaries. Healing can still be given to the horse by standing back and directing the energy where needed and by making any energetic changes to the horse's systems at a distance, or by way of it's aura.

After we have physically grounded ourselves and observed the horse and feel that it is ready for us to start, we need to connect to the universal energy. Just take a few deep breaths and ask that you be used as a channel for the healing energies to use, as they feel fit to do so. At this point you may start to see colours, you may feel heat, cold or tingling in you hands or even feel them being pulled towards the horse. There are no, right or wrong ways to experience these sensations. Some of you may feel that you are having nothing happen but this doesn't matter. As long as the intention is there so will the healing energies be there also. Now start to move your hands on or around the horse's body in an intuitive way until you feel that they need to rest in a certain area (some of you made find you intuitively go to a certain area straight away) You may find that your hands need to rest there for a while or that they need to move in that area a certain way. Just go with whatever feels right in this particular circumstance. When you feel that it is time to move onto another area just quietly and gently do so. A healing session may take ten minutes or it may take two hours depending on the individual and what they are in need of at this particular time. There are no hard and fast rules for healing and no two sessions will ever be the same. Keep moving around the horse using your hands in an intuitive way until you feel that the session has come to an end. Once this has been completed and you feel that there is nothing left to be done thank the horse for allowing you to take part in their healing and then reground yourself.

Energy Transference

As I have already mentioned, sometimes it is not always easy or right to get close to the horse due to past trauma or abuse. However it maybe the case, that there is someone that the horse does feel comfortable with and doesn't mind being touch by. This is another way that we are able to give direct healing to the horse. There are two ways in which we can do this. The first way is by asking the person trusted by the horse to hold them on a lead rope. We can then place out hands on that person if they feel comfortable with this and channel the healing energies through them with the intention that they reach the horse. Alternatively we can ask the trusted person to place their hands on the horse. We can then either place our hands on the person (if they feel comfortable with this) or even over their own hands and channel the healing energies again through them and out through their hands into the horse. Doing it this way means that not only do we still make a physical connection in an alternative way but we also allow the energies to pass through the trusted person also giving them healing and the experience of participation but we can also help them to connect with the horse on a deeper level.

Common Equine Reactions During a Healing Session

During a healing session not all horses will react the same way, but there are some common reactions that many horses show. Some horses may give just one or two of the following reactions whilst others may display many.

    Yawning
    Licking and chewing
    Rocking
    Lying down and going to sleep
    Fluttering of the eyelids or a sleepy expression
    Sudden aggression (release) and then relaxation
    Moving and weight shifting from different legs
    Moving so as to present you with another part of their body
    Bodily noises
    Lowering of the head
    Trying to move away from other people or animals close by
    Walking off, walking in a small circle and then coming back to you (Indicating grounding)
    A surprised expression and moving away (Usually whilst experiencing the new sensations being experienced or even a neigh to the person giving the healing or an equine friend)
    Resting their head on you or a stable door
    Licking you
    Sighing and/or letting out a long breathe

Please be aware that horses are large, strong animals. They are also prey animals that spend a lot of time in an alert survival state. Even when they appear calm and relaxed it is not uncommon for them to suddenly become alert and move quickly. If at anytime they feel under threat they may react suddenly so please be aware of this for your only safety and that of others at all times. Even a placid horse can change very quickly. Personally I prefer when safe to do so to leave the horse untied and for the healing session to take place on earth/grass rather than on a concrete yard. Of course there aren't always times when this is a safe way to carry out the healing session so each healing session, horse and environment must be taken on it's own merit and changed accordingly. But under no circumstances should healing EVER be inflicted on a horse that doesn't want it.

The Theta State

Most deep healing (and usually the longer lasting healing) will take place whilst we are in the theta brainwave state. This enables our mind to slow down a little and link with the horse's energies. Usually whilst in this state we enable the horse's brainwave state to also decrease so that it matches our own. Experiments have shown that deep healing will usually take place in this state compared with more alert brain states.

Grounding

Grounding as its name implies is to do with connecting to the ground or earth. Many of us lead busy lives and are focused on several things at once, which can cause lack of focus and a feeling of not being quite here in the present. The idea of grounding before we commence a healing session is to make sure that we are focused and our mind doesn't wonder so that we can give the session and the horse our undivided attention.

Grounding should always take place both at the beginning and the end of each healing session.

Protection

Some of you will have heard of the term 'protection' before. In simple terms protection is an energetic reality that we create to keep us safe from unwanted or negative energies that we could possibly come into contact will during a healing session. Protection is a very personal thing to use. Some may use it during each session whilst others choose not to use it at all. One thing I will add to this though is that if you do choose to use it do not over use it or become too obsessed with using it, as I have met some people that do energy work that have over used it to the point of being paranoid. They are so entrenched in using it from a fear basis that they actually make themselves feel unsafe when not using it. Fear has no place in healing, only love. Fear isn't a real emotion it is something that we create through paranoia or through past negative experience, imagination or lack of confidence. We have control over any fear we have, as we are the ones who choose to create it in the first place.

Some of the more common protection exercises involve enclosing ourselves in a golden circle of light. Imagining our self being showered with silver or golden rain as if being cleansed once the session is over. Or of putting ourselves into a one-way mirror shape that allows us to send out positive energy but not incur negative energy.

Another thing I would like to add at this point is what is positive and negative energy? And can one exist without the other? Whilst energy cannot cease it exist it can be changed. Each has their own individual meaning to each of us, they also have their own rightful place in healing. Quite simply negative isn't always bad as it can also mean balance or opposite.

Mental Energy Tools

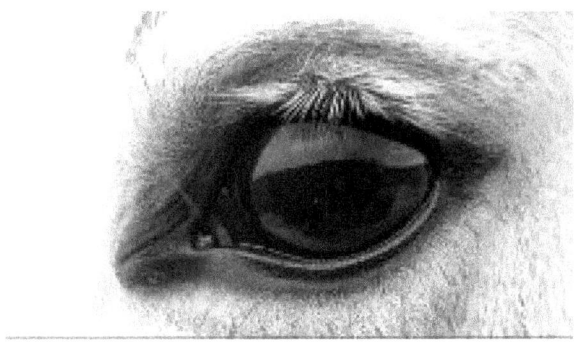

There are no limits to the type and number of energy tools we can use and create with our imagination. These tools not only help us access things quickly but also accurately. By accessing the horse before and after each healing session, they also enable us to see just how much of an improvement or shift has been made without having to go back through otherwise long winded checks.

Here are some examples of easily created energy tools that you may find useful within your work. Over time you will find and think of new ones to help fill up your tool kit. Once you become well rehearsed in using them you'll wonder how you ever worked without them!

The Energy Tap

This is one that I use to regulate the amount of energy coming through my hands. When working for the first time with a horse some may relax into the new sensations they are feeling, others may feel a little unsure. If they are feeling a little unsure I imagine my hand as a tap so that I am able to turn down the energy flow a little and regulate it to a flow that the horse is comfortable with. Once they have become accustomed to the new sensations I can then turn my 'tap' back up again to its usual flow.

The Sea of Emotion

This is a quick and easy tool to use when we need to access the horse's current emotional state. Simply close your eyes whilst keeping the intention in mind that you wish to see the sea of emotion for that particular horse. Bring to mind an open sea complete with sky. Now how does the water look to you?

Choppy – Unsettled emotions, frustration, nervous or agitation

Calm – Quite literally calm

Calm with a huge wave in the distance – Calm on the outside but repressed or soon to be expressed emotion (Is the wave moving any closer?)

Strong Currents – Different relationships, desires or people pulling them in different directions

Round current pulling in water downwards - holding everything in or a shutting off

Massive waves – Up and down and unsteady strong emotions

Calm with the odd little wave – Calm with the odd little upset

The Chakra Fan

I would normally use this tool within the charkas but it can be used for anything including the emotions. Imagine the blades of the fan turning in the chakra. Ideally at the speed a ceiling fan would turn.

Too fast – Strong emotion, head racing, too much energy

Too slow – Not enough emotion, weary/tired, lack of energy

Turning but getting stuck – Happy in general but with the odd negative emotion or worry.

The Sewing Kit

You can use your sewing kit as a needle and thread to quite literally stitch up holes and tears you may find in the aura, charkas and other energy systems, both in and surrounding the body.

Energy Putty

This is great stuff! Energy putty can be used for many different things. Most commonly to plug holes where energy is leaking out as this helps mend them and stem the flow.

Energy Blockages

If we imagine the charkas as vortices and the meridians as electric wires it is easy to see how they can become blocked. Sometimes you may come across stagnant or negative energy that is stuck in one fixed place, stopping the even flow of energy through that particular system. One of the easy ways that we can disperse this energy so that it begins to flow again is to imagine and therefore create an 'energy bullet'.

In order to do this all we have to do is imagine a silver bullet flying towards the energy and breaking it up. So that the blocked energy is able to disperse and start to flow again in a controlled manner. Whilst the charkas and meridians are common places to find such blockages they can be found throughout the body. Sometimes they are caused by emotional upset that is being held within a certain muscle. If this is the case finding and removing the cause of the blockage will help to release the muscle tissue, so that it is able to soften and circulation is then restored.

As you will already be aware horses hold a lot of emotion in their body through the stresses of everyday life. This can cause the muscles to contract and tighten pulling the skeletal frame out of place. Another way we can help with this is by gently massaging the muscles physically. This helps to restore the circulation to enable them to soften again. It is not unusual for a horse to react badly at times or at least to show some discomfort whilst you are doing this, as tight muscles are usually quite sore. The worse the reaction chances are the more sore the horse is, so please use any massaging of the muscles with caution and do it gently so that the horse can get used to it. Muscles that have a 'stringy' feel to them or feel knotted are usually muscles that have been contracted for some time and these tend to be the most uncomfortable.

Colours and Numbers

It is not usual for people that do energy work to see different colours when they are working or sometimes even numbers. Each colour and number will carry their own unique make up depending on the vibrations that they are made up of.

The colours are created by our own subconscious interpretation of what those colours and numbers mean to us, even if we don't understand them at the time. The aura has colours that are seen as pretty standard like the charka colours but that doesn't mean they are always right in the books. As each of us with interpret them in our own individual way. We don't always know or even need to know what they mean as long as we can see when change happens. It maybe the case that over time as you start to see these colours more, that you devise your own meaning for them which will short cut your work for you. As you will know what they mean when you come across them again.

If you see numbers then remember that numbers also carry their own vibration. It made be what you are seeing is a number scale - say for example you were seeing a tight muscle with the number six in it. If you are working from the idea that a soft muscle is a number one and a very tight and sore muscle is a number ten then you know that work needs to be done in this area. You can then view the number again once the treatment has come to an end to see if the number has lessened and if so by how much.

Energy Cords

Energy cords are a very interesting part of any healing session. They can be attached to any part of the body or any of the energy systems. Some people see them as coloured cords or pieces of rope or even octopus tentacles stuck to the horse with suckers. Again, this comes down to your own energy sight and interpretation.

When the horse is still emotionally attached to a past event, person, trauma or another animal, chances are you will find a cord that connects them to it. Not only this, but cords can be sent out to the horse by someone that has not let them go completely, or someone that is feeding off of their energy. Set your mind the task and intention that you wish to view any energy cords that are connected at this time. Firstly find where the cord attaches to the horse and then mentally follow the cord until you find what is at the other end. Spend a moment once you have found the sender or receiver of the cord and allow pictures and words to form in your mind to enable you to gain as much detail about what is going on as possible. Is this connection serving the horse? Does it feel right to disconnect the horse from what is at the other end of the cord? If the answer is 'yes', then follow the cord back to where it connects to the horse. Gently cut or detach it and allow the cord and what is at the end of it drift away with love.

Sometimes it may be the case that although the horse needs freedom from whatever they are attached to, they might not yet be ready to let go. If this is the case then leave the attachment firmly in place and start to investigate why the horse isn't yet ready to let go, so that you can enable it to work towards a time when it is. Needing separation doesn't always mean right now! If you have disconnected any cords then just take a quick look to make sure that no open holes have been left and if you find one stitch it up or why not put some of your energy putty in there!

Chakra Balancing

Chakra balancing is a good way to give a standard healing session. Once the charkas have been brought into balance it enables the emotions and associated parts of the body to also find their full energy level, this is a basic and straightforward treatment, it is also a very important one. If you are planning to give the horse several healing sessions over a period of time it is usually a good one to start with. This will give a good, solid foundation for the rest of the healing to sit on.

Firstly, start at either the crown or the root chakra, which ever feels right to you. Either feel the energy of the chakra with your hands or use your energy sight to view it. What does it look or feel like? Is the energy strong or faint? Does the colour look bright and vibrant or dull and muggy?

Place your hands over the chakra whilst asking that whatever divine healing that is needed be brought into the chakra. You should start to see the appearance or feel the chakra start to change. Once you feel this has been completed simply move onto the next chakra and work your way through them, one by one until the healing session is complete.

Trauma Blasts

These tears at times can be quite big. They look as if they are a shining white or silver energy coming from the body and can often be felt from several feet away. These are rare but can be symptomatic of major trauma to the horse's energy systems.

The horse's own energy systems can become so overloaded or thrown so out of balance that they quite literally have huge energy blasts that have ripped their way out of the horse. The biggest and most damaged blast I have ever seen is that of a horse I was asked to give healing to. She had previously suffered forty minutes of being electrocuted by a mains line. She was very luckily to survive as I have yet to hear of another that has survived such a major electrocution. Unfortunately the mare was wearing a metal bit in her mouth that just made the problem worse. The energy leaking from her was coming from a hole in her side about one by two feet round. It was so strong that I could feel it from eight feet away, as it was quite literally pouring out of her. After I spent some time patching up the hole, the energy was hardly leaking anymore and could only be felt two inches from her body.

Problems arise when these types of issues are not recognised and the unknowing healer will channel energy endlessly to the horse. Soon as the horse is receiving it, it just leaks out again making much of the healing session less beneficial.

Water Vibration

Water is very much a living energy. All water carries its own vibration that can vary depending on its individual source and what it has come into contact with along the way. A Japanese doctor by the name of Masaru Emoto has carried out in depth studies on water vibration. What he has found is that when a droplet of water has been frozen it forms either the shape of a snowflake or a distorted shape. He found that the droplets of water that formed the beautiful snowflakes had come from sources such as holy wells, natural streams and rivers and water that had been prayed over. The distorted shapes came from water sources that had been contaminated in some way such as mains water and dirty rivers. Further more he preformed tests that showed that it was actually possible to change the vibrational formation that the water droplet made. This was done by placing positive energy near to the water or standing the water on it in a suitable container. The positive energies that he used came in the form of: pleasant words, gentle or classical music and prayer.

Being as the horse's body is made up of around 75% - 90% water it would stand to reason that the thoughts, feelings, intentions and environmental factors around the horse, play a huge role in how the water in their bodies reacts vibrationally.

There are many ways in which we can use these discoveries within the healing of horses. It could be as simple as just keeping tabs on our thoughts and words we use. When we are around the horse and the love that we feel for them, or by changing their water in their water buckets to a more 'digestible' vibration.

Chakra balancing is a good way to give a standard healing session. Once the chakras have been brought into balance it enables the emotions and associated parts of the body to find their optimum energy level. This is a basic and straight forward treatment that is also a very important one. If you are planning to give the horse several healing sessions over a period of time, it is usually a good one to start with as it gives a good solid foundation for the rest of the healing to sit on.

Firstly, start at either the crown or the root chakra, which ever feels right to you. Either feel the energy of the chakra with your hands or use your energy sight to view it. What does it look or feel like? Is the energy strong or faint? Does the colour look bright and vibrant or dull and muggy?

Place your hands over the chakra whilst asking that whatever healing is needed is received. You should start to see the appearance or feel of the chakra start to change. Once you feel this has been completed, simply move onto the next chakra and work your way through them one by one until the healing session is complete.

If we imagine the charkas as vortices and the meridians as electric wires it is easy to see how they are able to become blocked.

Sometimes we will come across stagnant or negative energy that is stuck in one fixed place stopping the even flow of energy through that particular system. One of the easy ways that we can disperse this energy so that it begins to flow again is to imagine and therefore create an energy bullet.

In order to do this all we have to do is imagine a silver bullet flying towards the energy and breaking it up so that the blocked energy is able to disperse and start to flow again in a controlled manner. Whilst the chakras and meridians are common places to find such blockages they can be found throughout the body. Sometimes they are caused by emotional upset that is being held within a certain muscle. If this is the case by finding and removing the cause of the blockage another way will help to release the muscle tissue so that it is able to soften and circulation is then restored.

As you will already be aware horses like us hold a lot of emotion in their body through the stresses of everyday life. This can cause the muscles to contract and tighten pulling the skeletal frame out of place. Another way we can help with this is by gently massaging the muscles. This helps to restore the circulation and enables them to soften again. It is not unusual for a horse to react badly at times or at least to show some discomfort whilst you are doing this as tight muscles are usually quite sore. The worse the reaction chances are the more sore the horse is, so please use any massaging of the muscles with caution and do it gently so that the horse can get used to it. Muscles that have a 'stringy' feel to them or feel knotted are usually muscles that have been contracted for some time and these tend to be the most uncomfortable.

Readings the Horse's Aura

If you are able to see energy and the horse's aura when looking at it, or even in your mind through using visualization this is a good place to start for gaining information about the horse. This can be information about its past, health and emotional issues as well as past life injuries and trauma.

Exercise

Either stand with the horse or visualize them in your mind. Now look for the colours of the aura and where you see these. You don't need to know the text book meanings for the colour as they will have different meanings for different horses. Write a list of which colours you are seeing and where. Now sit quietly with your list, keeping each colour and area in mind as you read it and spend a few minutes asking the horse what the colour relates to for them, as an individual.

Natural Healing and Other Therapies

Crystal Healing

Crystals are used a lot with healing for horses. There are literally hundreds of different crystals that have been mined from all around the world. Each of these crystals depending on its type will carry a certain vibrational healing property as well as, its own unique blueprint. The correct crystals are selected and either held against the horse, left to rest in their aura or charkas or left in their close environment such as a stable. The horse is then able to absorb the frequencies that the correct crystals transmit.

Essential Oils

These oils are very strong and pure as they are extracted from the actual oils of the plant. There are hundreds of oils that we can use in Equine Aromatics. These oils as well as having a physical make up also carry vibrational qualities making certain ones wonderful for different types of negative emotional states. Many of the oils also have nutritional qualities. The wonderful thing about oils is that the horse is hardwired to recognise what the body needs so is able to self-select the required oils as and when needed.

Please be aware that some oils can burn the skin and others are toxic so they should always be used by a professional so as not to cause any harm. If you were interested in studying this subject I would recommend reading 'The Animal Aromatic Handbook' by Caroline Ingraham.

Other Energy and Natural Therapies

Here is a list of commonly used therapies that you may well find useful to aid the horses that come into your care. All of these therapies can be worked with in a 'text book' or intuitive way, the latter often being the most beneficial to the horse. Many but not all therapists have an element of energy work within their therapy depending on their own level of understanding and advancement.

Chiropractic

This therapy involves the gentle manipulation of the body to help realign the spinal column and other parts of the skeletal system. Sometimes this can take several treatments in order for the bones to stay in place because the muscles must be strong enough to hold them there. If the horse has been misaligned for a long period of time the muscles would have adapted to holding the body in this new way. It can take twenty-one days for the muscles to reform and be able to hold the body into its new and correct alignment.

Homoeopathy

The idea behind homeopathy is that when using it we are treating 'like with like'. The disease or illness held within the body will hold a certain vibrational signature unique to that illness. The idea being that by treating the body and energy systems with the 'same' vibration the vibration is then cancelled out.

Like all therapies and medications that are energetic in nature homoeopathy should only be used by those who are very experienced and educated it its uses. Currently it is only legal for a suitably qualified veterinary surgeon or the horse's owner to prescribe such remedies for a horse.

Herbs

It is believed by many people that for each illness or disease there is a natural plant source to help combat or alleviate the problem. Each herb used has a medicinal property, that when used correctly and in the right dose can help the body to correct itself, release toxins or provide itself with the nutrition needed. Herbs have been used for many thousands of years in Chinese Medicine (and by horses) with amazing results.

Horses have an inbuilt intuition as to the healing ability of herbs and when left in a natural environment they will often be seen self-medicating. When we make herbs unavailable to horses within their everyday environment we then take away the choice for them to self medicate. In the case of grazing horses pastures are best left naturally without the use of weed killers, as much of what we view as weeds is medication to our horses.

Example

Chamomile – Calming and soothing

Milk thistle – A good liver tonic

Dandelion – Helps support the urinary system and liver

Plantain – Similar properties to linseed

Spiritual Healing

This therapy involves the Healer, (or channel as they are often referred to) channeling Chi (Life Force Energy) into the horse. This maybe carried out by touching the horse or by holding the hands slightly away from them. Energy is then channeled from the universal energy source into the Healer and out of the palms of their hands towards the horse. The energy will then find its own way into the physical and energetic parts that it needs to reach. Spiritual Healing can also be carried out at distance in much the same way.

A more commonly known form of hands on healing is known as 'Reiki'. It is believed that the ability to heal or channel healing energies is passed down from 'Master' to student through a series of 'attunements'.

Radionics

This therapy is sometimes used with what is termed 'the black box'. The idea being that the horse's energy systems are read and deciphered and any blockages or abnormalities are dealt with by sending the correct vibration signal to put them right. This therapy in past years was given little credit but more recently it has become much more widely accepted. As with many other therapies it can be used not only for correcting health problems, but also with maintaining good health so it may also be thought of as a preventative. In recent years it has become commonly used in the competition horse world.

Colour Therapy

After assessment of what the horse needs the practitioner will select the correct colours for the horse that will give off the required vibration. These colours (though not always) will be bright, often similar to the colour of the chakras. They may come in the form of internal stable walls painted a certain colour to the correct one selected for a water bucket or even a rug.

Chakra balancing is a good way to give a standard healing session. Once the chakras have been brought into balance it enables the emotions and associated parts of the body to find their optimum energy level. This is a basic and straight forward treatment, it is also a very important one. If you are planning to give the horse several healing sessions over a period of time, it is usually a good one to start with as it gives a good solid foundation for the rest of the healing to sit on.

Firstly, start at either the crown or the root chakra, which ever feels right to you. Either feel the energy of the chakra with your hands or use your energy sight to view it. What does it look or feel like? Is the energy strong or faint? Does the colour look bright and vibrant or dull and muggy?

Place your hands over the chakra whilst asking that whatever healing is needed is received. You should start to see the appearance or feel of the chakra start to change. Once you feel this has been completed, simply move onto the next chakra and work your way through them one by one until the healing session is complete.

If we imagine the charkas as vortices and the meridians as electric wires it is easy to see how they are able to become blocked. Sometimes we will come across stagnant or negative energy that is stuck in one fixed place stopping the even flow of energy through that particular system. One of the easy ways that we can disperse this energy so that it begins to flow again is to imagine and therefore create an *energy bullet*.

In order to do this all we have to do is imagine a silver bullet flying towards the energy and breaking it up so that the blocked energy is able to disperse and start to flow again in a controlled manner. Whilst the chakras and meridians are common places to find such blockages they can be found throughout the body. Sometimes they are caused by emotional upset that is being held within a certain muscle. If this is the case by finding and removing the cause of the blockage another way will help to release the muscle tissue so that it is able to soften and circulation is then restored.

As you will already be aware horses like us hold a lot of emotion in their body through the stresses of everyday life. This can cause the muscles to contract and tighten pulling the skeletal frame out of place. Another way we can help with this is by gently massaging the muscles. This helps to restore the circulation and enables them to soften again. It is not unusual for a horse to react badly at times or at least to show some discomfort whilst you are doing this as tight muscles are usually quite sore. The worse the reaction chances are the more sore the horse is, so please use any massaging of the muscles with caution and do it gently so that the horse can get used to it. Muscles that have a 'stringy' feel to them or feel knotted are usually muscles that have been contracted for some time and these tend to be the most uncomfortable.

The Human and Horse Link

Have you ever bought a horse that was the opposite to what you intended to buy? As if for some unknown reason you were drawn to that particular horse and couldn't get them out of your thoughts? Or have you ever met someone else's horse and had a familiar feeling that you had met them before?

This is a very common thing that I find with Equine Therapists. As if there is some kind of unspoken connection between them and the horse that they have recently met. It can happen for one of several reasons. Firstly it may be that there is a past life connection between you and the horse. Or it maybe that you recognise them on another level and that there is healing to be done between the horse and yourself. Or an experience or learning that needs to take place. Lastly, it could be that your energies and emotional state resonate with the horses like a tuning fork vibrating. causing the resonation of those other nearby energies to resonate at the same frequency, as they are so alike.

Whatever the reason, the strong connection between some horse's and their owners or other people, close to them cannot be denied.

For some years now the horse has been playing a leading role in the healing and connecting of their human friends, similar to the dolphins and how they choose to interact with people and heal them. I firmly believe that the horses have chosen to take on this role as they are so easily accessible to humans and that, many of us are able to encounter them in our day-to-day lives. If you ever come across such a feeling be sure to take notice of it and follow it up, as if you don't you may well be missing out on a valuable piece of the puzzle. See if you can find out just where that connection lies and what you need to learn and experience from it. These types of relationships cannot only be very beneficial to all involved but also very nurturing and loving to those that are lucky enough to come across them.

The Owner and Riders Influence

Have you ever thought one thing but voiced it as something else? A typical example of this would be when someone asks you how you are feeling and you tell them that you are 'well' or that you are 'fine'. When in actual fact the total opposite may apply to your present state of mind or way of thinking. This is why horses can become very confused by us. Not only are they hearing or feeling a contradiction from us but also, we are contradicting ourselves through the minute signals that we maybe giving off physically. The horses are easily able to read this by observing our body language and the changes in our energy.

I have come across countless cases to date of these kinds of problems arising and often these are the cause of undesirable behaviours that the horse may display through their frustration or confusion. A typical example of this would be someone that has been 'bucked' off by their horse and now is nervous due to that experience. The next time they climb onto their horse they maybe feeling nervous but are trying to convince, both themselves and their horse that they feel confident. Whilst externally they maybe showing confidence their body will be giving them away through the minute signals that they give off, if even only through their raised heartbeat. They then feel that they are telling their horse that they are in control of the situation and what is happening and that everything will run smoothly. Inwardly and subconsciously they may be terrified and part of them is secretly hoping that the horse will buck with them again. Although this might be a scary event for them if the horse were to buck it would then give them a good reason to dismount and not get on the horse again. Thereby avoiding the scary situation and not having to do it again. A rider that is scared of riding in a faster gait or a rider that is scared that the horse will bolt again is also a common problem that can also bring about the very situation that they are trying to avoid. Jumping a horse is also another typical example, especially if the rider is secretly or subconsciously hoping that the horse will run out at the jump, as they themselves are scared to jump.

The Horse's Emotions

From what I have witnessed to date, horse's emotions are no different to our own. They still have the same level of complex emotions and depth of emotions that we experience in our everyday lives. Science tells us that the horse has near enough the same emotional chemicals that we do. These are usually referred to as the neuro-peptides. Not only are these emotional chemicals found in the brain but also throughout the body. When we stop and think just how much our stomach area and our digestive tract is affected by emotional upsets it is easy to see why horses are so easily effected in the same area of the body, due to having such a large area of digestive anatomy. These chemicals can also be found in the heart of a horse as well as other organs of the body. They have the ability to love, grieve and reason, just as we do and their emotional state and ability to experience emotions should never be underestimated.

When a Horse is Very Ill or Dies

This is a very emotional time for all involved but often it can also be a happy time. None of us like to see an old animal trying to hang onto its life by the threads. Or a long suffering horse that has been neglected in a field for months when it should have been 'sent on its way' long before.

In an ideal world when the time comes for our dear equine friends to leave their physical bodies behind they would just close their eyes and drift off to sleep, waking up in a better place. Sadly this rarely happens so it is often the case that the decision needs to be made in order to help them on their way to prevent further suffering. The chosen option for this is often the horse's veterinary surgeon though some owners do opt for the local huntsman. There are two ways in which this can be done. Either by shooting: Using a gun, or by lethal injection. When lethal injection is used many vets will opt for sedating the horse first. Occasionally some choose to send their horses to a slaughterhouse. This is not a dignified ending for any loyal friend. The horses can at times be handled roughly. They do not have people they trust near them, they are able to smell the stench of death all around and can be stood queuing for long periods of time until their fatal time has come.

There are pros and cons to each of the two above methods. With shooting it is very final and very quick. One minute the horse is here and the next it isn't. The speed at which their soul is 'thrown out' of he body can be disorienting for some. For other more spiritually aware horses this method can be good, as they know exactly where they are going and how to get there. Obviously from a 'viewing' situation this can be traumatic for the owner and any other people that witness the ending of a horse this way, it is not always a pretty sight.

Injection is often a little less stressful as usually the horse will become quiet once sedated and will just stand for the lethal injection to be administered. Most will then just slowly fall to the ground and their heart will stop beating soon afterwards. Sometimes there maybe slight movement of the body or labored breathing but most of the time things will go smoothly. There is the odd occasion when things don't go as smoothly and a second injection needs to be given as the horse fights against it or their circulation is poor. My personal theory on this is that being as the subconscious runs the horse's body there are times when a horse is put to sleep when it knows it needs to stay, in order to complete something or as it can be healed. That in some cases it is literally a case that the horse is fighting to stay which of course they can't with shooting. Please be aware though that this is not always the case and that physical issues can also play a part in a slow passing.

It can be a very distressful situation when we are asked to give healing to a horse to 'make it well' when we can clearly see that the horse is literally begging to go. In such a situation the horse's vet should always be involved and their advice listened to. Of course it is normal for owners to want their horses fit and healthy again but ill health and age is just part of life's ongoing cycle that we cannot stop from happening. Giving healing to a horse that is about to pass on can be very beneficial to help them pass safely and peacefully. Knowing that they are in the hands of people that care for them and they trust. It is very important that when healing is given, it is given for the horse's highest good. This means that we know we are not sending the wrong energies out and trying to hold the horse in a body that it just doesn't need anymore.

Owners will express their emotions differently during this time. Some will be very upset even to the point of having second thoughts. Whilst others will put on a brave front and do their crying in private. Though for some this can take some time as they choose to repress the emotion, rather than express it because this for some feels safer. However they choose to express themselves give them reassurance that there was nothing more that they could have done and that they have made the right choice. As for some owners this will have been one of the hardest decisions they have ever had to make in their life.

For some people, their horse is a part of their family. Or in some cases even a replacement for a child. Many of these owners would have lived their life daily with their horse for as many as thirty or even forty years. This is a very long time to have a close friend and then to loose them. By the same token the feelings within the relationship between horse and owner can be just as strong sometimes even after just a few weeks of their partnership beginning. The bottom line is loss is always hard, when we are parted from something or someone we love and grieving needs to take place in our own time and in our own way.

I once heard the saying 'not a life cut short but a life well lived' this is something I often remind my clients of. In many cases it's not so much about how old the horse is, so much as has the horse lived out their life? Have they done what they needed to do? Experienced the things they needed to and spread the happiness and healing they so willingly gave? If the answer to this is a 'yes' then without a doubt the horse lived its life to the full.

Support for the Owner

Having a horse with severe psychological or physical problem, or a horse that is near death can be a very emotional experience for the owner. Many of the people that you will come across will have searched out behaviourists and those in the medical profession, to no avail. Very often as healers we are the last ditch attempt for many owners that have already explored all of the other options available to them.

People handle their own emotions in many different ways. There are those who become very upset and cry and there are those at the opposite end of the scale that have become seemingly angry through pure frustration. Due to everything they have tried in order to help their beloved horse not working. However they choose to express themselves we must always keep in mind that any anger expressed or any frustration is not truly aimed at us, but rather at the situation they have found themselves in. At all times how ever hard it may be we must enable ourselves to see things from the owner's perspective, learning to understand their underlying emotions that may be causing the anger. At all times we must maintain a professional approach but also be open to understanding their emotional side and empathise with it, but at the same time not allowing ourselves to be emotionally drawn into their drama. As if we do this we can loose our concentration and not maintain a clear head in order to focus on the presenting situation.

As an Equine Healer you will find that much of your work is also with the owner in times of crisis or upset. By helping the owner to understand the situation and by supporting them, you will be able to help them to stand back from the situation and gain a better, balanced perspective. Their horse needs them to be strong at this time and you, will be able to help them to reach inside of themselves to find their hidden strengths. If you thought equine healing was just about horses, think again! In order to help horses we must help their owners too. As the owners play a huge part in the day to day life of the horse. The better balanced emotionally the owner is the more beneficial they will be to their horse.

Integrity and Mental Focus

Without a doubt your level of integrity will not only play a part in how you conduct yourself outwardly and towards others but will also, have a huge affect over the horses that you work with. In any vocational work of this kind money needs to change hands in order to keep the balance, or alternatively another type of swap involving work or time. It is when our ego and drive for money becomes out of balance that we are doing not only ourselves but also the animals that we work with an injustice. No matter how well we try and disguise how we feel, the horses will know our true intention and this alone can make or break a healing session. If you do not feel comfortable to the horse then no doubt it will feel uncomfortable in your presence.

Most of us will be leading busy lives in between our healing work and will have problems of our own that weigh on our mind. It is very important to understand that when we commence a healing session our problems must be left outside of the stable door or field gate. So that we are able to give the horse that needs us our full attention. When we allow our mind to wonder onto other things the horse can feel uncomfortable and our integrity can go out the window along with our thoughts and concentration. For this reason it is always advisable to ground yourself both before and after a healing session is carried out.

Munchausen Syndrome by Proxy

Munchausen by Proxy is a mental illness whereby the sufferer uses their animal (or child) to gain attention for themselves. Usually the person in question will have something missing from their life that is fulfilled (or seemingly so) by receiving attention from other people. By physically or energetically maintaining their animal's illness they gain people's pity and attention that then enables them to feel better.

Many people who have this disorder on a physical level are aware that they are doing it though they may not always be sure of the reason behind it. They will usually know it is wrong and yet are unable to stop themselves. People who do it on an energetic level are usually totally unaware, although not all. Similarly people can drain an animal of their energy as a way of boosting their own rather than choosing to channel it from elsewhere.

Symptoms of Munchausen Syndrome by Proxy

The owner (or another person) administering the horse with knowingly harmful foods or medications, usually on a regular basis.

The owner who chooses not to get medical attention, that the horse needs.

A person who pushes their horse out in front of them, using them to hide behind. By people noticing the horse the owner will then be given attention without them having to make it obvious that, that is their aim.. Also an owner who continuously talks about their horse to the point that they loose friends as there is no other topic of conversation.

People who take their horse from vet to vet, and from therapist to therapist claiming that, no one has been able to help them but they know that you are 'the one' that can. Usually this will involve the changing of many vets and therapists over short period of time so that the relevant people aren't able to have long enough to treat the horse, with any chance of success.

The owner who says that money is no issue and then spins a very long tale about how much they love their horse and how much money they have spent on them with no improvement seen. This may even be over a span of quite a few years.

The owner who telephones you anytime of night or day, trying to gain as much sympathy from you as they can with their woeful stories of how things aren't improving with their horse.

Obviously some of these symptoms can be totally genuine with no cases of Munchausens behind them but more often than not, when three or more of these symptoms are shown, there will be an element of the problem existing.

When someone is harming their horse in such a way it can be very distressing for us as an outsider looking in, as we feel helpless to do anything. In the case of physical harm being caused we can notify the relevant authorities. With the energetic form of this mental illness there is not much that we can do to help unless the horse's owner chooses to recognise that they have an illness.

In order to stop the horse's owner from draining us in the same way we need to back step a little and approach the whole situation in a professional manner. So that we don't find ourselves caught up in the owners self made drama. It can be very hard to help a horse in these circumstances as on an energetic level, as whatever we do to help will be counteracted by the owner. One thing that we can do is wrap the horse up in golden healing light to help keep them safe. Then explain to them that we understand about their situation and that we are always open and willing to listen whenever they need us.

Those who have a good understanding of mental illness and are good at talking and interacting with people maybe able to take this a little step further. Try engaging in conversation with the owner about themselves. By dropping certain things into the conversation at the required time, it might be that we can bring the horse's owner to a certain understanding about what is going on. If they are able to accept this it may well be that they choose to look into counseling or a therapy to help them with their problem. Usually this is the best and in many cases the only way to help horses that unfortunately find themselves in this kind of situation.

Types of Aggression

There are several different types of aggression that can be displayed by horses; here are some of them you may like to familiarise yourself with.

Aggression in order to protect their off spring. - In the case of past or ongoing abuse, fear of abuse, or attack.

Assertive Aggression – This type of aggression is associated with dominance induced aggression or territorial aggression.

Mixed Aggression – As it indicates this can be a mixture or two or more aggressions rolled into one. Such as fear aggression, coupled with assertive aggression.

Stress Induced Aggression – At times this may also include redirected aggression, such as in cases as when a horse is feeling frustrated so it kicks out at another horse. For no obvious reason as it's just redirecting its aggression in order to release it.

Pain Induced Aggression – This is a very common aggression seen in horses.

Inter-Male (or female) Aggression – This type of aggression tends to be when two males or females sets out to attack or dominate the other in order to take on the role of herd stallion or alpha mare.

Whenever we see signs of aggression it is important for the horse's sake that we correctly assess which type of aggression that it is. Some displays may just be a natural behaviour that needs to play out if safe to do so. Such as inter - male/female aggression, whilst fear based aggression or pain induced aggression should never be overlooked or punished.

Stallions

Sadly for many stallions they are forced to live in lonely stables. Often away from other horses on the yard and many receive very little, if any turnout. For many people 'owning a stallion' may be seen as a bit of a status symbol, so some choose to keep their male horses entire for the sake of it. Others of course choose to keep them entire for breeding or as tease stallions, one of the saddest affairs of all. Tease stallions tend to be stallions that haven't made the grade for breeding so are kept in order to bring mares into season, so that the breeding stallion can then cover them. In saying this in my visits to yards I have come across stallions that are real gentlemen and live out with geldings or young colts. I have also come across stallions that live in bachelor herds. (Not ideal but then again this often also happens in the wild as there will only be one stallion to a herd of mares and youngsters. Meaning. there are often many stallions left without herds that choose to form their own) I have also come across two cases of vasectomised and therefore, still able to cover but not breed, stallions happily living out with a few chosen mares. Interestingly both of these stallions were Arabian as were many of the bachelor herds. But as we have already mentioned for many stallions it can mean a lifetime of loneliness and isolation. Some colts mature individually more quickly as do certain breed types. The youngest colt I have so far come across that has sired (fathered) a foal was eight months old. Yet my own Arabian colt was happily living with his mares without any problems, until he was fourteen months old. From this it is easy to see why there are so many cases of stallions that are hard to handle and have emotional and psychological problems. Many colts are removed from the herd once they start to show signs of wanting to cover (mate) with mares, or when showing aggression. They tend to either be isolated or put with other young colts or geldings. Many of these horses are still young and because of this, are still needing the influence of a strong lead mare or mother figure. This will enable them to learn how to behave and to live in harmony within an established herd.

When we create single gender herds like this we can create unbalance. As the males and females of the herd often have different roles to play within that herd in order to set up a healthy balance. Also in order to breed top class stallions, a lot of interbreeding goes on as well as selected and single trait breeding.

The problem with single trait breeding is that when we select two animals to pair up to bring about the outcome we hope for. The offspring we breed can often be left without the important other requirements that are natural, or at least should be natural to that horse. This can even be as relevant as having mistakenly breeding out the 'courting of the mare' in a stallion's behaviour. That instead turns him into a raging rapist, though it might mean he comes out it with a nicely shaped head for showing!

Whatever the reason for keeping a horse entire, the horse's future must be thought through. As often colts or stallions that are 'late cut' may still retain much of the stallion behaviour. Even to the point that some may still try to cover and even damage mares or be hard to handle. It is not uncommon to come across stallions that are only walked out in a 'chifney' (a nasty strong type of anti rear bit) or with a bridle and curb chain (a curb chain is a metal chain that runs under the back of the lower lip and pulls tight when the stallion pulls against the handler). This is no fun for them nor is it fun to suffer day in day out with raging hormones that they just can't control.

Some stallions that aren't used for covering cope very well and are easy to handle, due to the type of environment they are kept in. It is very sad for those that live their days out in dark stables hardly leaving them. Some not even seeing proper daylight from one week to the next, that never even experience grazing grass. So with this in mind is it any wonder that so many stallions suffer from behaviours, such as self harming? (Biting themselves repeatedly being the most common) Out of sheer frustration over their own life and why so many display other types of unnatural behaviour.

The Alfa Mare

The Alfa mare is the title given to the mare that is the leader of the herd. The lead mare's role is to take care of the needs of the herd. She makes sure that the whole herd runs smoothly and often helps to train the young foals and horses within that herd. From my observations there are two types of Alfa mare:

The True Leader

This is the type of mare that doesn't need to bully or threaten other members of her herd. She has gained respect from the lower ranking members through consistency, fairness and natural air of authority. She proved herself worthy of such a position through her conduct.

The Enforcer

This type of mare bullies her way to the top, by creating fear of injury and emotional fear in low ranking members of the herd. Usually the apparent respect she has earned to gain this role is actually a false respect and may, more genuinely be viewed as the horses bowing down to her through fear of attack of her hooves or bared teeth. These mares aren't quite ready to take on such an important role and will often suffer from stress and having to constantly discipline younger members of the herd that are growing in dominance. As they see fit to challenge her weak status. It is not unheard of for a true Alfa mare to also bow down to such a mare. This is done so that the true leader that is actually still the leader of the herd may retain harmony within her herd. She does this by fooling the enforcer into believing that she is still running the show, thereby avoiding conflict. True leaders do not feel the need to fight. Their air of natural authority, confidence and dignity with which they conduct themselves says it all.

Early Weaning

The right time for weaning has always been something of a debate. Many people think that six months is old enough, some think a year. It may also be argued that there is no 'right time' and that weaning has nothing to do with age of physical maturity but rather with emotional and mental maturity and self-confidence. Many different breeds of horse physically mature much more quickly than others, this can be a little misleading from the point of view that a horse that 'looks' older is older so often is better expected to cope with the weaning process. The truth of the matter is that 'imprinting' (learning from the mother) can often go on as long as four or five years when left to do so naturally. Though this isn't often seen in wild herds, as it is usually the case that the mare falls pregnant again so at the time her previous foal reaches the age of around one she begins to push it away.

There are also many different, viewpoints on how weaning should take place. Some people feel that by removing the foal swiftly and placing it with other foals and the dam (mother) with other horses is the kindest way. As not only do they have company to occupy themselves, but that they are out of 'earshot' so can't hear one calling the other. Though the question needs to be asked in this case that just because the calling stops more quickly is this the kindest way? After all, how does one know what has become of the other and does their 'silence' actually mean 'forgotten' or just given up hope?.

Many also choose to wean when they first see the dam start to push them away. It is common for this to be seen as the start of the dam rejecting and weaning her foal herself. From personally witnessing this I would argue that this is the beginning (and I mean beginning) of the foal learning what life is like on the outside. A little like a human child, starting nursery when mum stands back and lets them play. But does the child not run to mum for reassurance? Some mothers leave their child to cry until they 'get over it' but does getting over it mean they actually do?. Or that they just learn to cope through distraction? Further more what goes on in their child's mind when this is taking place?

A large amount of foals are weaned early for financial gain. Many people love to have a new 'cute' foal not thinking what has taken place in order that they can have them. Would it not be better to let that foal learn and grow, with it's dam and move permanently away from mum when mum ceases being mum and becomes a close friend/another member of the herd?.

A huge amount of emotional problems such as insecurity in horses even as old as their twenties and thirties comes from early weaning. When buying a foal we should all be aware of what has taken place in order that we may be happy. If people stopped buying such young foals, there wouldn't be such a market for them. In short, the longer the foal is left with mum and better still weaned by mum the chances are the better mentally and emotionally developed that foal will be in later life.

The Horse as a Prey Animal

As you will have already noticed prey animals have their eyes set on the sides of there heads and predators have their eyes at the front of their face. When we look at how the prey and predator hunt and are hunted and the scenario works. It is easy to see why they have evolved this way as the predator needs his focus on what he is hunting up ahead of him and prey animals need to have a larger visual band in order to see stalking predators, as they creep closer before it is too late.

Of course, these days our domesticated horses don't need to worry about lions leaping at them out of the hedge whilst out on a ride. But as far as I am aware no one has explained this to them yet! But joking aside, saving and preserving themselves from hunters is still a natural and innate instinct to them. This would be largely taught through mixing with other older horses from a very young age that is passed down through generations. Though I suspect there is a strong element of inborn instinct at the time of or very soon after birth. We can see how the horses have evolved to deal with this by being able to run literally hours after birth in order to save themselves from becoming 'dinner'.

Sadly as this instinct still remains very strongly so in many horses, they are constantly looking over there shoulder so to speak. These horses can in some cases be permanently on guard which causes them to be stuck in the flight/fight mode or stuck on the 'in breathe'. Though of course there are a huge amount of happy and relaxed horses out there that will flee for their lives through something as simple as a carrier bag, that is flapping in a hedge that may just be waiting to leap out and bite them on the nose.

Stuck on the 'in breathe' or stuck in fight/flight mode means that, the horse is on guard, getting ready to run if it needs too. This is a very stressful state for the horse, that can lead to weight-loss, bolting, (running away with the rider) and 'edginess' as well as holding in a breath and alert like stance. From an energetic point of view these horses will undoubtedly be ungrounded and would greatly benefit from being reconnected to the earth.

Self-Harming

Unfortunately, self-harming isn't as uncommon in horses as we would like to think it is. It usually takes the form of the horse biting itself but can also show itself in other ways such as repeatedly banging legs until they bleed. The problem with such behaviour, that stems from frustration at the situation the horse has found itself in, can also become habitual. Once it has become an established habit it can be much harder to stop. The golden rule here is to assess why the horse has become so angry and frustrated in the first place and try and change the environment, husbandry or whatever else is wrong for the horse. To enable the horse feel as safe as possible. Giving healing will help to disperse some if not all of the negative energies that are playing out. but finding the reason for the behaviour in the first place is paramount. Self-harming means that the horse is taking it's frustration out on itself by turning it inwards rather than outwards. So again we must assess why this is going on and why the horse feels unable to express itself in another way.

Often the cause is years and years of repressed anger through isolation, such as a lone stabled stallion that is unable to 'touch' the rest of his herd, but not always. In such an instance it will be a case of having to use good observation skills to be able to determine what is going on and how best to change the situation so that the healing is able to be fully effective. It is all very well for us to balance the energies involved.. But if the underlying cause is still present, the issue is likely to reoccur.

Holistic Horse Management

The word 'holistic' basically means the 'whole' (wholistic) So in this case we are referring to the whole horse chemically, mentally, emotionally, structurally and spiritually. In order to take all of these things into consideration we must assess the horse's life as a whole. This means everything from its companionship, to living and turn out area, to its food and natural forms of self medication (such as herbs in the field), its work, the people who look after and care for it, to other therapists, rugging, and hoof care.

The Barefoot Horse

Keeping and riding a horse without metal shoes is becoming more popular as people are starting to see the benefit. The hooves are designed to walk many miles a day over terrain best suited to the breed. In order to do this successfully the horse needs to be regularly trimmed in a way best suited to the individual. Environment also plays an important role as keeping a horse in a wet muddy field that softens the hooves and then expecting it to be able to carry you over stony ground, isn't always possible.

It is a sad fact that due to how we have chosen to breed some horses, they may struggle on hard or stony ground due to poor hoof quality and conformation. In these instances we need to ask ourselves what we have done to them to change their natural capabilities or indeed are we asking too much of them? When they were a foal they managed to run and play without shoes, why should that change?

These images show healthy hooves.

Notice the roundness of the hoof, wide heels and nice wide frog.

Rehabilitation

Rehabilitation in basic terms means helping to change something about the horse that isn't in its best interests, to enable the issue to heal. This can come in many forms. Horses may need rehabilitation for their hooves, behaviour or ridden work or various illnesses Usually the idea of rehabilitation, is that it is used in a holistic way in which hopefully, all of the horse's needs are taken into consideration.

We know only too well how the horse's physical body as well as its emotional state can affect just about everything about the horse. So we need to get the horse functioning properly in all levels in order that it can be as happy and healthy as possible. This will no doubt play a vital role in sorting many of the horse's problems. Rehabilitation for some horses just literally means being turned out into a field for six months to a year, or even more in some cases just so that they can learn to be a horse again. Enabling them to be a horse again, have thinking time and a well deserved rest.

The way in which many horses live or are trained, can become so ingrained that we inadvertently train them out of being who they really are. Even to the point that they become emotionally switched off and robotic, unable to make decisions for themselves. It is vitally important that the horse be able to make some (safe) decisions through their own thought processes. When the horse becomes too reliant on the owner or trainer it can become very insecure when then left to its own devices. It is not unusual to see a horse that has been institutionalised almost emotionally break down when it is left to not only make its own decisions but also given a more natural life style. Often it is a case of the bigger the breakdown the bigger the past control in life style.

The Horse's Eye Sight

As a prey animal a horse has excellent long distance vision. This enables them to see predators at a distance in order to give them time to flee. Whist horses also have good short vision they also have two 'blind' spots. These are two to three feet in front of them and behind them. Because of this 'flapping' arms can easily distract some horses that are feeling unsettled or are new to riding. For some horses cyclists coming up behind them can also be a problem. This is due to the narrowness of the rider and bike. As they move about or as the horse moves forward the cyclist can move in and out of the horse's vision, causing them to disappear then reappear as if by magic.

The blind spot in front of the horse can also present a problem. It is hard for them to see objects coming into their immediate head area. This is especially so for horses that have been hit and abused, especially those that have been hit around the head. Vision can also be a problem with water and jumping. Horses have a hard time judging depth. This is why jumping poles are usually set up at jumping level and one lower down in bigger jumps, under the main pole, where a pair of poles, are crossed. This enables the horse to access the depth between the two, in order to enable it to know just how high to jump.

Water can also pose a problem for them when it comes to judging depth. How do they know that when they step into the puddle it isn't going to swallow them up to their necks?! Reflection in water can also distract and unsettle horses, especially in sunny weather when reflections may be present.

Equine Seasonal Affective Disorder (ESAD)

ESAD is a type of winter depression that affects a large number of equines every year. Mostly between September to April and in particular during December, January and February. It is caused by a biochemical imbalance in the hypothalamus due to shortening of daylight hours and less sunlight reaching the back of the eye. For many horses ESAD can be a seriously debilitating illness, preventing them from functioning and focusing normally. For others it can be milder but still a debilitating condition but causing discomfort rather than serious illness and suffering. Vitamin D can aid this issue and is absorbed through the skin from daylight. So removing rugs and sunny winter days may be seen a beneficial in some cases.

The Horse's Soul

As previously discussed the horse's soul plays an important role in who they are. Each horse like us, has a life path that needs to be followed. Sadly by the decisions that we often make for them we can steer them away from this. Many horses rather than just being a riding horse, pet or companion have other roles in life that needs to be fulfilled. These roles may include being a healer for others or a teacher. By allowing them to fulfill their role when they are emotionally and physically ready to do so, we enable them to move forward spiritually, as well as physically and emotionally. The horse has an inner knowing of exactly what that role is and when unable to carry it out frustration and behaviour problems can occur.

After the horse's physical death the soul will leave the body and journey to the after life. Here it will take time out to reflect on its life and rest before moving on to another body. This is what is often referred to as reincarnation. Another scenario that may take place is that the horse's soul by mutual agreement with the existing soul, may take over the body of another horse that is already in existence, on the earth plane. This process is referred to as a 'walk in'.

Horse Vices

'Vices' are the name given to label certain unwanted behaviour that a horse may show such as:

Wind - sucking – The holding onto a stable door or a fence and pulling back with their teeth whilst gulping in air.

Cribbing – The chewing of fences and the top of stable doors and similar.

Weaving – Moving the head from one side then the other in a swaying action, whilst moving from one front foot to the other.

Box Walking – The walking past a stable door or, gateway then immediately turning round and doing it again. Rather like the pacing that cages large cats do in zoos.

Whatever kind of vice a horse may be showing the chances are that the original cause was stress. When a horse engages in this behaviour, the endorphins, the bodies own 'feel good' chemicals are released from the brain. This is why more often than not when the horse is using this behavioural pattern it will have a 'switched off' look. Or appear completely focused on the behaviour despite what may be going on around them. The problem with vices is that they can become very mentally ingrained.

Once the original cause of the stress has been removed, the horse may well carry on this behaviour purely for the feeling it gives, or as a habit. It is not uncommon for a horse to not even really be aware of this behaviour, as it has become so automatic. A bit like people who tap their fingers on a table or bite their nails without realising it as they have been doing it often and for so long.

Endorphins

These are the feel good chemicals or natural pain relief chemicals that are produced by the brain. They are released when the horse becomes injured or ill and is in pain. They are also released through the engaging of vices and will create relaxation in the horse.

Natural Horsemanship

Natural Horsemanship has been around for along time but has become far more popular in recent years. Unfortunately natural doesn't always mean 'natural'. In some forms of training gadgets are still used to try and stop unwanted behaviour, instead of getting to the root cause and dealing with it accordingly. It is advisable to study as many of these training methods and trainers as possible so that you can form your own opinion. Sadly many trainers that use 'Natural Horsemanship' choose to take on the role of the enforcer mare rather than the passive leader, unsettling for the horse and arousing it from its calm state. I have watched some trainers and how they observe the horse's body language and use their understanding of it to control the horse. Pushing them so that their adrenaline levels rise, causing them to feel threatened, so that they are looking for way out. Unfortunately the answer they usually arrive at is 'how to survive' rather than actually understanding what the trainer is asking for. So compliance is given but not for the right reasons.

For many trainers this will bring the desired response but to detriment of the horse. I have also watched other trainers that take on the role of the true Alfa mare. They work quietly and passively. The horse's stress levels do not rise or if they do it is to a very low level. This method tends to be the preferred choice of horses as it is less stressful to them and more 'natural'. As in the wild with an alpha mare as their trainer it would be less likely to lead to injury or even fatality. Of course we can make a horse move through waving our arms around, but wouldn't a polite 'ask' suffice? When done this way we can gain true respect of the horse and the chances are your request will be met with the correct response.

Nutritional Requirements

Healing is not a substitute for nutrition. Just because you are giving healing to a horse that may have physical problems, it doesn't mean that all of its requirements are being met. Nutrition plays a huge role in the health of the horse and when deficient it can cause a broken down nutritional pathway. This means that if the horse is lacking in one thing it may cause of chain reaction of mal-absorption in other areas as well. Good feeding practices will rule out many such problems in this area. Many breeds have developed different nutritional requirements due to where they originated from, though much of it does stay the same. It is not unusual for the debilitating problem referred to as 'sweet itch', which is when the skin becomes flaky, dry and itchy for the horse to be found to be low in selenium, Vitamin E or both, as well as an abnormal immune response.

Toxins

The liver is the organ that is responsible for cleaning the body of toxins, along with the kidneys Due to the external toxins often digested by the horse in the form of weed killer, poisonous plants, wormers and other drugs. The liver can sometimes become a little overloaded. By keeping the horse's environment clean and not over using chemical wormers, we can help to eliminate part of the livers workload. Drinking lots of fresh water will also help the body to flush out toxins.

The Equine Star Chakras

As well as the main charkas that are in the horses energy system, there are also many others. These include the star chakra s that are also often referred to as the transpersonal chakras. These work with the horse's connections not just to mother earth but also to their connections 'above', 'spirit' or 'source'. Depending on which word feels most comfortable to you.

You may see them as differently as described here but I have included the general colours that we are aiming for. What you may see or feel maybe different, as the horse's energy systems like our own are personal to us. Please do be aware as with anything to do with changes made to the horse's energy systems. It is not about what we the Healer want to see change wise for the horse. It is about the horse's own self empowerment and want for change and improvement that is important here. When we change energies we can also change the life path of the horse, as well as current and future lives and even the energies passed down to offspring. Please bare this in mind and be sure that any changes you make energetically, in any form are in the horse's best interests. Also that the changes that you are making are being asked for and the horse is ready to accept them.

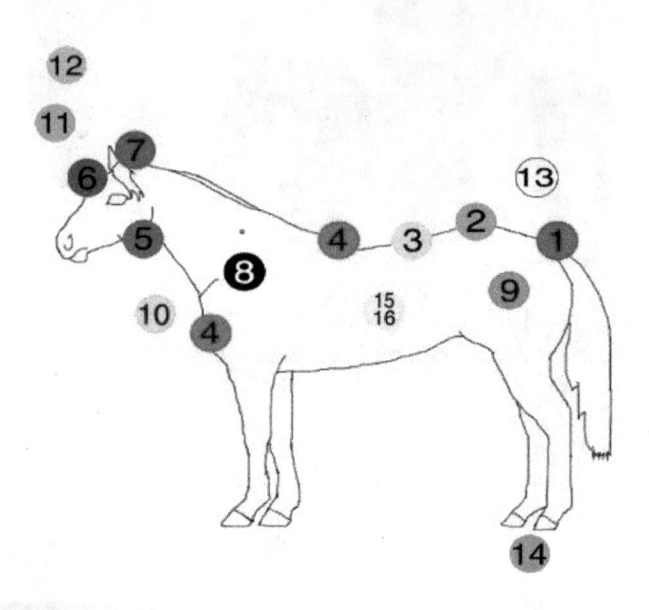

1. Base - B
2. Sacral - S
3. Solar Plexus - SP
4. Heart - H
5. Throat - T
6. Third Eye - TE
7. Crown - C
8. Brachial - B
9. Second Heart - SH
10. Thymus - TH
11. Soul Star - SS
12. Stellar Gateway - SG
13. Home Star - HS
14. Earth Star - ES
15/16. Balance Left/Right - BL/R

Earth Star

This is situated below the horse's hind hooves. The correct colour is generally the earthy colour khaki.

This is the grounding point that the horse will use when they earth their energies. It is their connection to Mother Earth and helps to keep them firmly 'rooted' physically in this incarnation. Being properly grounded through the Earth Star helps the horse keep it's subtle bodies anchored and aligned correctly. Horses that are flighty or easily scared or timid may well benefit by being correctly anchored by this chakra, having it opened and fully developed.

Soul Star

This is situated about one foot above the head and slightly forward. Its colour is generally silver when it is open and healthy.

It is the bridge between impersonal essence and personal reality. The soul star works as a transducer to moderate the very high vibrational energy and information brought down from the spiritual planes, through the Stellar Gateway, to a level that the horses can assimilate in their physical existence. It also enables a good connection to self.

Stellar Gateway

This is situated above the Soul Star. The colour generally associated with this charka is gold.

Once it has been activated it is the horse's direct line to the Divine Source. The connection needs to work both ways, as a spiritual exchange between the horse and the Divine Source. It enables access to infinite energy. It enables a detachment of the heart and mind and from the personal. This enables the horse to see the clearer picture and not to become too wrapped up in the physical details of everyday life. It enables them to see things how they are and come to the understanding of why things happen the way that they do. It also brings about a greater understanding not just of life, but also of relationships and the world as a whole.

Home Star

This chakra is situated about twelve to eighteen inches above the body between the sacral and base charkas. It's colour when open and healthy is generally seen as white.

The home star connects the horse to its original origins. When the home star isn't fully functioning the horse may feel disconnected and alone. It also enables the horse to remember who it is and why it is here. The opening and connection to this chakra may also bring about a feeling of contentment in the horse. As they know that no matter how far away from home, they are still connected to their origins.

Balance Left & Balance Right

This chakra is situated each side of the horse and best felt about two metres away from the actual body. If one or both sides become blocked they need to be cleared so that the shadow side of the horse may connect with all of it's other energy systems to enable it to turn it to light. The shadow side of the horse is everything we see personality trait wise that we may think of as being negative. But on the contrary, within each negative also lies a positive.

Healing Through the Bladder Meridian

The bladder meridian is a meridian that allows us easy access to the other meridians. This meridian starts above the horse's eye, runs over the poll (the poll is the top of the horse's head) then, runs along side the horses neck and spine about 3-4 inches from it in a line. It then turns slightly, coming down the backend and running down the outside of the horse's hind leg. When this meridian becomes blocked or the energies in it are not running smoothly. Not only is this meridian affected, but also other meridians can be as well. Making this makes a prime way of accessing other energetic parts of the horses system.

Ill fitting, saddles that sit across the horses wither can also cause blockages to this meridian.

What we are looking for once we have found and are treating the blockage is the following sequence: Firstly locate the energy blockage – Hold your hand there – Wait for the response from the horse to show we are in the correct area – Then wait for the release in the form of licking and chewing, fluttering of the eyes, letting out a breathe, general relaxation.

In order to treat any problems in this area start by putting you fingers or your hand just above the horse's eye. Then gently use it to slowly trace alone the meridian all the way to the end of it at the coronet band just above the hind hoof. This needs to be done slowly so that not only can you feel for any blockages in the meridian, but also that you can watch for any physical reactions from the horse. These might be slight reactions such as blinking when you come to a blocked area to larger reactions once you reach the hind leg and hoof such as the horse picking up it's hoof or shaking a leg. Different horses react in different ways and some will be more subtle than others.

Once you have found a blockage, hold your hand or fingers over that area. Imagine pouring in light healing energy until you feel that the even flow has resumed. Then move along the bladder meridian to see if you can find any further blockages. Once you feel that the bladder meridian has been cleared. You can then move around to the other side of the body and work your way down the bladder meridian on that side so that both sides are working fully and together.

Etheric Light Crystals

This is another technique that is very versatile and easy to use, in many different types of situations. These crystals aren't physical as they are made up of pure white light. In order to use them and bring them in, just visualise yourself holding them in your hands and they will appear with practice. They can be used in a variety of ways including:

Using a small piece of the light crystal broken down into small particles to place in or cover an injury.

To stand inside a blocked meridian or chakra to help open up the flow and remove the blockage.

For putting particles of crystal into your healing putty that is used to plug up holes and tears in the horse's energy system.

Basically anything else you can think of, as the opportunities are endless!

Epilepsy in Horses

It is believed by many therapists that unresolved and subconscious emotional issues cause epilepsy. This can cause the neurotransmitters (the brain chemicals) to miss fire, stopping information to be passed on through the brain. Those therapists that are able to see energy in and around the body often see this as a 'sparkler', type energy in certain affected parts of the brain. It is also not uncommon to see a silver or white line running from the brain into a part of the body such as a limb. This may be showing that the muscular response in the limb or other part of the body in which it is seen is being affected. Sometimes this may show as an uncoordinated movement or a slightly slower physical reaction in that area of the body. By working through and resolving the emotional issues, more often than not this problem can be corrected.

It is also not unusual for the horse to take on emotional trauma on behalf or the owner, or another person close to them. It maybe that when the issue is resolved in the owner, that the horse also no longer has the problem either. So in any cases of epilepsy in horses it is advisable to first look into any emotional problems causing it and to find out if it is in fact the horse's issue or the owner's.

The Horse's Past Lives

Many therapists believe that we come into existence as purely an energy form. Then when we are ready, we choose a suitable body to be born into so that we can learn, experience and grow spiritually. Usually encountering life lessons along the way. It is believed that not only is this the case for people, but also for horses and other animals. After the life has been seen through, hopefully the relevant experiences and lessons that have been experienced by the soul will then pass from the horse's physical body over to the 'other side'. Or the 'Summerland's' as it is often referred to. Here the spirit will review it's life and see what it learnt and didn't learn from that life, time so that it may assess what still has been left unfulfilled.

The horse's spirit may then decide to return to the earth to experience the lessons it failed to learn in its previous incarnation. Or even new lessons in order to move it forward on its spiritual path of evolution. Often it is the case that horses need to experience or repay karmic debts with other people or horses with which it may have wronged previously. Been wronged by, or didn't teach or learn from the last time around. For this reason it is not usual when first meeting a horse, to feel drawn to them as if there is a familiar feeling about them. This is often experienced as a 'knowing' that you have met before. This may be your own horse or even one belonging to a client. Sometimes there will be lessons to work through or experiences to be had. Sometimes though, all that is needed is an acknowledgement that you have recognised each other again. For the therapist this may stir up feelings or memories from a past life that we may then recall, either on a conscious or subconscious level. We can then work through these and analyse our own healing, as well as that of the horse.

The Horse's Present Past life

Due to the subconscious memories and feelings the horse may have brought through from its last life. Or even life times previous to that, it is often the case that they will end up with certain people. It may be that the person who bought the horse that you have been asked to see (or even a horse you bought yourself) actually set out to buy, an entirely different type of horse. Then for some reason, usually due to a subconscious recognition, they were drawn to this particular horse and chose to buy this one instead. For some people this can be a very strong feeling and just an intense knowing of 'I know this is the horse for me'. This can also come about through an energetic resonance of 'like attracts like', when the horse's energy matches that of the potential buyer.

Once we have been able to establish why this meeting between horse and therapist or horse and owner needed to take place. We can work through the healing needed so that the past is able to stay in the past where it belongs. The horse can move forward freely with ease of mind. Also bear in mind that in some cases there will not be a past life connection but more a case of 'like attracts like' and the horse and owner needed to come together. This helps to aid in each others healing due to their emotional issues being so a like.

Past life problems in horses are very common and cause them to bring through emotional trauma and upset to the present lifetime, in order that it may be healed. Such subconscious upsets can easily lead to phobias and unexplained and irrational behaviour and fears. By clearing through and working through the past life issues that are affecting the horse in this lifetime we are able to help them to move forward.

The Horse's Life Path

As with all animals and people, horses have a predestined path, or rather a path that they are *meant* to follow. When this correctly plays out for them it means they will get to experience the things that they are meant to. Learn the life lessons that they came here to learn and come into contact with the people they are meant to form relationships with. Sadly this isn't always the case as all too often humans have a part to play in throwing a spanner in the works.

This might come in the form of an owner who knows that they need to give up their horse. They have done all that they can and the horse needs to move onto the next person, in order to experience still further. Yet the owner is unable to come to terms with letting the horse go. By the same token it could be that the horse is ready to pass over to the other side. As it has experienced all that it needs too but that the owner selfishly still needs them to stay as they love them too much to let them go. Though in these cases it is highly questionable as to if the person does actually truly love their horse as if they do would they not let them go?

Often horses come into our life not for their own need to experience, but for ours. It may be that you find yourself taking on a horse that is ill. No matter what you try and what veterinary treatment may be used it is all to no avail. In such circumstances we need to stand back and assess just what exactly is going on here. May be this is our lesson and just about coming to terms with the fact that we can't save all horses. No matter how much we want to and no matter how much we think we need them to stay with us.

Past Life Injury and Trauma

During past lives that can take on many forms such as horses that were previously horses or even horses that were humans. There will at some point be trauma caused by an emotional or physical event, or both. These traumas will then affect the horse's aura or blueprint in the form of an energetic disruption. These weaknesses in the blueprint when left unresolved can then be brought forward in their energy systems into the present day. It may even be the case that the weakness in the blueprint was caused many life times ago. This may have caused physical injuries or emotional problems that keep repeating themselves and have been experienced through many life times.

The Horse's Blueprint

The horse's aura may be seen as the blueprint for the physical body. That is to say that in order for physical change to come there must also be an energetic change. Once the energetic correction is made it then leaves room for the physical body to repair where possible.

Think of the aura as the overlay for the physical body.

The Original Trauma Line

As we have explained above, these traumas in whichever way they occurred can be carried through many life times. In order to correct the trauma in the here in now, we need to trace back to the original trauma and deal with it there. If this isn't done and the trauma from only the most recent past life is addressed a level of weakness will continue to remain in that area. Until all of the traumas from past lives that have happened in that area of the body have been resolved.

In order to find where the problem first started stand with the horse. Or if this isn't possible, picture them in your mind. Look at the area of the body where the physical symptoms are showing and ask the horse in your mind to show you when the first trauma happened. In order to do this try visualising a line coming from the blueprint or the physical body in the area of weakness. Watch how long the line is and how far back it goes. Ask the horse to show you the image from that first time so that you may understand what has happened to them in able to help them to heal. Once they have shown you ask them if they feel ready to be disconnected from the link made to this time. If they are not yet ready then leave it alone and write it in your notes so that you can address the issue again at a later date. It might just be the horse needs further healing before it is ready to let it go. If however the horse feels ready to be disconnected from these past injuries and trauma. Gently detach the line from their aura or their physical body with your hands. Coil it up and give thanks for what you have been shown. Then hold you hand out palm facing upwards with the coil in it. Asking that it be taken with thanks as it is no longer serving the horse a purpose. Then ask the divine energy to lift the coil from your hand that it may transmute it, as it is no longer needed.

Lost Soul Parts

In extreme cases of trauma it is not unusual for 'part' of the horse's soul to leave the rest of it. In order to explain this fully we may find it easiest to view the soul as a puzzle. Interlinked and slotted together as if made up of lots of different parts. Once trauma happens one of these parts leave the rest and goes to a place where it can emotionally detach from what is going on. This happens as a way of the horse avoiding mental and emotional collapse. Whilst this is good in one way it also means the horse ends up with part of itself missing. If the horse's soul is not complete then the horse is not complete.

Exercise

Try visualising the horse's body as a jigsaw puzzle and look for any pieces that appear to be missing. Once you find one look into the gap that it has left as deeply as you can, to see how far the part has retreated. Whilst we may be looking into the horse's body or energy field in order to do this. It is often the case that we find ourselves looking into a gap filled with something else entirely. The missing piece may be seen as the horse in another existence and another body. Or it may be the horse in this lifetime during the time the trauma happened. Whatever part of the horse it is that you can see. Ask in your mind for that piece of the horse's soul to return if safe and right to do so. It may feel a little apprehensive about this, not really knowing if it is safe to return even if it needs to. Explain to it that you will enable it to come 'home' and help it link with its other parts so that it can fully integrate. To enable the horse to be who he needs to be. You may find that if the soul fragment has been gone some time it might need a little help to find its rightful place back into the jigsaw puzzle. If this is the case you can work with visualisation or your hands to enable it to find its rightful place, back within the horse's energy systems.

In some cases it is not unusual to see the horse sigh at this point or lower its head or show some other kind of release. Showing that trauma has been released and the soul fragment returned to its rightful place.

The Golden Energy Loop

The golden energy loop is energetically drawn with either the hand or the fingers. It may also be visualised as if drawing it with a crayon or similar. It is in the shape of the figure of eight and is a good tool to have in your healing box. This figure of eight loop is symbolic of eternity. It can be used as a valuable tool for quick healing when there is not time to do a complete session. We can 'draw' the symbol in the energy field or straight onto the body where it is needed. Or even around the whole horse once the healing session has come to an end. This helps to 'lock' the given energies into place.

In cases where horses seem a little disconnected physically as if there backend doesn't know that their front end exists. It can also be used as an energetic bandage to encourage the horse to move correctly. In order to do this we draw the symbol as if applying a stretchy bandage. This goes around the horse's chest, up towards it back, crossing behind the withers then coming to rest around the horse's seat bone area. By applying this way not only are we applying the healing that will help with horse but also giving it an energetic training tool to help and encourage it. This enables the horse to be aware of both its front and back end, where the energetic bandage has slight but comfortable pressure. Whilst encouraging the horse's hind legs to come underneath their body in order to raise their back.

Another application of this of course can be a physical bandage. Though if doing this please make sure that it is not too tight and that it is made from a stretchy fabric in order to bring the best comfort to the horse.

The Basics of Dowsing

The basics of dowsing involves, asking a selected question and using the dowsing as a way of finding the answer. It can prove invaluable when we feel unable to gain an accurate answer by another method. So that we can work as openly and honestly as possible. It is important to take a 'detached' view of our work without the underlying want for a certain answer. Or to have any personal gain outside of integrity attached to that answer.

When dowsing we must have an open but enquiring mind and try not to be biased as to any particular outcome. Getting to the point of unattached curiosity however comes with time and patience. When we choose to ask a question during dowsing, we are asking and searching for that question using our logical mind. Whilst we wait for the answer to be given to us we must adopt a state of being unbiased as to the final outcome, in order that a truthful answer is given. The answer then comes back to us very quickly in the form of a movement by the tool, (Either a pendulum or dowsing rods) with which we are working.

Types of Dowsing Tools

There are several different types of dowsing tools that people choose to use. The most popular tend to be the Y Rod, the L Rod, the Aura Metre and the Bobber as well as, the ever-popular Pendulum.

The movement of the preferred tool occurs through minute movements in the dowser's muscles, commonly referred to as a neuro muscular response (NMR). However being as the muscular movements are so faint. It would appear to the dowser that the rod or the pendulum moves by itself. The action of the muscular response is an involuntary movement not consciously controlled by the dowser. This movement happens naturally without any effort. The more we relax the more forthcoming the movement by way of response.

The Pendulum

This tends to be one of the more common tools of choice due to it being small (unlike dowsing rods it will easily fit into any pocket). It is easy to make your own pendulum using something as simple as a key, or a crystal on a piece of string. However there are some very nice pendulums for sale so buy one that you feel drawn to. It gives its response by spinning in circles, side to side, diagonally or forwards and backwards.

The Bobber (or wand)

This is one of the more traditional dowsing tools that in the past was often made of hazel twigs. It consists of a long piece of metal or a slim twig about 12-15 inches long with a weight on the end. By holding the handle at the other end a response is given by the weight at the other end 'bobbing'.

The Y or V Rod

This too is a very popular tool that tends to be used a great deal by mineral and water dowsers. It consists of a V shaped piece of plastic, wood or twig (often hazel or apple wood). Whilst the V shape faces away from you the other two ends are used as handles. It gives its response by way of the joined end (that points away from you) pulling up or down.

The L Rod

These rods are most popularly used for searching for things such as earth energies and locating other similar energies. They are easy to make out of something as simple as an old wire coat hanger. First bend it so it has a right angle then cutting it so that one end is about 3-4 inches long and the other end is about 5-8 inches long. The smaller length ends are then used as handles. They give their response by either swinging open when held parallel.or, by closing across each other, or even by spinning round and round.

How does Dowsing Work?

Dowsing works very easily. We simply have to ask a question clearly to which the answer can either be 'yes' or 'no'. All we then have to do is wait for a response to come back to us, giving us our answer.

When first learning to dowse the most commonly used tool of choice tends to be the pendulum. As it is so versatile and convenient being as it can be made of basically anything to hand. For now we will discuss starting off by using the pendulum. Then in time you may like to consider moving onto working with rods so that you have the chance to become fully equated with both sorts of tools.

The movement is made by what is known as a neuro muscular response. This involves the brain or mind connecting to the answer and sending small electric signals to the muscles in order to cause a slight movement in the arm. This is so subtle it will not usually be seen or felt.

Using a Pendulum

Firstly hold the cord or chain of the pendulum between your thumb and first finger of your dominant hand. Hold it in such a way that your finger and thumb are pointing downwards. Then allow the pendulum to swing forwards and backwards. This is your neutral swing position, meaning that you are ready to ask questions. Make sure that you have as little tension as possible through your shoulders and arms. The longer the pendulum cord or chain, the slower the swing is. By shortening the cord a little you will increase the speed of the swing, allowing you to have a more responsive reaction by way of an answer. There is no set correct length for the cord but usually a cord or chain of around five to six inches is the most popular.

To start, sit comfortably with your pendulum swinging. Then ask either out loud or in your head that you be shown a 'yes response'. It is always important when asking questions that you have a clear mind and ask directly. Take note of how your pendulum in swinging to show you your 'yes'. It may be swinging in a circle, from side to side or diagonally. But whichever one it is you can now take this to be your 'yes' indicator.

Now allow your pendulum to return to its neutral forwards and backwards swing. Now repeat the process as before but this time asking for your 'no' response.

By now if you are unable to achieve any movement for your 'yes' and 'no' indicators. You may want to check that you are relaxed and that you aren't holding any extra tension in your upper body. Especially your arms and your shoulders and then try again. It is not uncommon to have no response the first time we try dowsing. Remember we are at this point trying to connect with a part of ourselves that many of us haven't been a touch with for a very long time. Remain patient and if you feel yourself getting a little frustrated just put your pendulum away for a short time. Until such a time when you are feeling more relaxed.

Now that you have established your answers for your 'yes' and 'no'. You are well on your way to gaining almost instant answers to important questions. Take time to experiment and you will be able to use your pendulum in a variety of interesting ways.

Typical Pendulum Responses

Anti clockwise for 'no'

Forwards and backwards for 'neutral'

Clockwise for 'yes'

You may find that you have another variation. This is fine so long as your 'yes' or 'no' answers are consistently the same. Although any deviation from above is likely caused by a blockage in your energy systems somewhere.

Directional Dowsing

This is an exercise that works well with both the pendulum and the L rods. It is a good for establishing reactions made by you through your tool of choice.

First hold your pendulum in the 'neutral' position. Now decide on a point in the room such as a door or a window and ask that the pendulum show you where it is. You should find that your pendulum swings forwards and backwards, side to side or even diagonally as a way of pointing this object out to you.

Refining Your Newly Found Skill

Now that we are well on our way to using our pendulum in a skilled manner, we can start to use it within our day-to-day life. One way that we can do this is by making charts. By setting the pendulum in a neutral position we can then hold it over the chart to gain a correct answer, when there are several possible answers. We can also work in the same way with lists. Also moving it down the horse's legs or spine and asking for a response when we get to a problem area.

Advanced Pendulum Responses

Now that we have spent some time working with our pendulum it is time to advance a little on our responses. This will help us to have more definite answers when a simple 'yes' or 'no' isn't quite accurate enough.

In order to do this we will work the same way as when we were looking for our original 'yes' and 'no' responses. Here are some that you might like to try.

Anti clockwise oval 'no but'

Clockwise oval 'yes but'

Side to side 'answer unavailable'

Clear your Mind and Connect

Start you pendulum in a neutral position and then ask to be shown 'yes'

Ask if it is the appropriate time and place to ask these questions (permission)

Dowse the required questions clearly and simply

Ask if you then need to be asking any more additional questions at the time that surround the subject

State the conclusion

Ask if it is the truth

Give thanks

Working with Non-Attachment and Appropriate Timing

As we have commented on before, whilst asking dowsing questions it is very important to make sure, that we are not attaching our selves to a particular answer. As if we do it is possible for us to influence the pendulum into giving the desired answer. This then of course is by no means accurate

Whilst there maybe answers to questions that we are wanting to find, it may be that it is not appropriate for us to know the answers, or perhaps it is not the appropriate time. Many questions can be answered but not all. This can be due to the fact that certain answers might divert us from a particular life path that we are not yet ready to stray down. Or it could be that it is simply the case that some things need to be thought through logically or emotionally and a conscious decision made about them. Learning to accept that we can't have the answers to everything is part of what makes us professional dowsers. This is due to the fact that it is very easy to get carried away in the excitement of it all. Just step back a little and allow your intuition to do its work, with no interference from the ego. Just allow the pieces of the jigsaw puzzle to fit together, as you go along.

If you are feeling tired or emotional about something, it may be best to dowse your questions when you are feeling a little more clear-headed. Or even ask someone else to do it for you, if it is something that needs sorting out within a certain amount of time.

If you are feeling tired or emotional about something, it may be best to dowse your questions when you are feeling a little more clear headed. Or even ask someone else to do it for you, if it is something that needs sorting out within a certain amount of time.

Blind Dowsing

There will be times when we encounter questions that we feel need to be asked, but we can't be entirely sure that we will not influence the answer. There is a dowsing technique that can be used to help combat this referred to as 'blind dowsing'. Make up pieces of paper with possible answers written on them to include, 'yes' and 'no'. Make several of each then shuffle them so you no longer know which is which. Lay them face down so that you are unaware where each answer lies. Ask your question clearly and then dowse over the pieces of paper each in turn. Once you have a positive response to one of the pieces turn it over to see what your answer is.

When you first start to work with blind dowsing it is advisable to first try using it with 'test' questions. This is a good way of checking your accuracy before proceeding with your important questions. By using this technique, we are unable to influence the given answer through our own desires for a particular answer.

Earth and Environmental Energies

As well as naturally occurring earth energies and those redirected by sacred places and standing stones. There are also other types of energies that can present a problem to the horse. This can be something as simple as a new horse with a different kind of energy entering the herd to, electric pylons and telephone masts. All of these have the potential to upset a sensitive horse and its energies. This can sometimes take away the potential for them being able to ground themselves.

Horses experiencing these kinds of problems may complain of a tingling, in their hooves that goes up the legs and into their body. Or maybe a feeling of dread, when they enter into a certain field or stable. The type of symptoms felt will usually give us an idea of what kind of problem it is. For those of you that can see energy, it might even be that you are able to see how the horse's energy is being distorted by these energies. Grounding the horse may help in some instances but more often than not crystals maybe used to aid in the protection of the horse from such energies.

Grounding the Horse to the Earth

Many Equine Therapists will use the base chakra to ground the horse to the earth. This is all well but we can aid the horse further in its grounding, by enabling it to ground to the earth star below the hind hooves. By grounding it to this chakra point we enable them to connect right to the center of the earth. In order to do this we must first check the energies of the earth star chakra to see if it is already functioning fully. If it is then it is just a case of connecting the energy from it to the horse's hind hooves and legs, if not already connected. This can be done by pulling the energy up from the earth star and down from the horse's hind legs and hooves. (Or even from further up the body, if the energies of the horse are higher up due to be largely ungrounded) and reconnecting them. If however the earth star is not activated you will need to put vital energy into it, as a way of helping it to function. Once this has been done the reconnection can take place as above.

Symptoms of a horse that isn't grounded properly can be agitated behaviour, spookiness and fretfulness and a general problem with the horse not being able to relax.

Connecting the Horse to Home

When the horse isn't properly connected to their own individual 'home' they can feel lonely and not feel comfortable in their own skin, as if just having been 'put here' and expected to cope on their own. By reconnecting the horse to its original home we can aid them in feeling reconnected to it. As well as to the earth through the previous exercise. This enables the horse to feel connected in both ways so that they feel comfortable being here and with who they are. In order to achieve this we work much the same way as we did in the earth star exercise. Only this time we use our intention to connect with the energies of the horse's 'home'. By pulling these energies down and the energies of the home star chakra upwards, to enable them to reconnect.

Divinity in Horses

Due to the horses having the stellar gateway chakra they have a direct link to 'source'. Once this chakra is open and functioning correctly this enables them to see the bigger picture of their life, and that of others. As well as enabling them to access higher knowledge. Many believe that the horses are either taking over from the dolphin's role or working along side them with humans. This is most likely due to the fact that horses are more easily accessible to people than the dolphins are. This can easily be seen by the recent rise of interest in Equine Facilitated Healing and Equine Facilitated Learning in the last few years. This is now so common in the USA that many insurance companies now accept it as a valuable form of treatment for people.

Horses play an important role in enabling us to learn about who we are. Not only that, but also to see how we treat each other and treat other species as well.

It is through this connection that some horses are so very humble and tolerant., putting up with just about anything that people dish out at them. We see cases where some horses can't cope and emotionally switch off' whilst others just go with the flow and tolerate us. The latter usually happening due to the opening and connection through the stellar gateway. As this enables the horse to understand that whilst their situation of what is being done to them may be uncomfortable, they also are aware of a higher reason. As well as the role that they have within this which to a degree enables them to cope. As they understand that this is a large part of their life's work. That we humans are just on a learning curve and they are our teachers.

Working with the Second Heart Chakra

When horses take on the role of healing humans, they do this by connecting to their second heart chakra, which is located in their flank. The colour of this chakra is pale green. When it is open and fully functioning they are then ready to take on their role as a healer for people The chakra enables them to connect with the person's emotions and energies so that they can view them in full. How many times have you witnessed someone hugging their horse's bum? Chances are this is a subconscious act on behalf of the owner in which they are choosing to connect with their horse in this way through their chakra.

Metal Shoes and Bits

Like metal shoes, metal horse bits can also pose a problem for the horse. Some of you may have experienced problems with sensitive teeth when trying to eat chocolate bars that have, been previously wrapped in foil, or when drinking hot or cold drinks. Metal bits can pose a similar problem with some horses resulting in tooth sensitivity.

Metal shoes and bits can also conduct electricity. So for horses that are very sensitive to energy in whatever form, they may have a problem with this. The having to cope with metal nailed to their hooves or in their sensitive mouths can prove quite a problem in some cases. Metal shoes in some horses can also cause a problem with grounding. In much the same way as having an energy treatment can when the horse is stood on a concrete yard. Though this is not to say that metal shoes and bits pose a problem in all horses, it is something that you should be aware off when making your assessment of the horse and its presenting symptoms.

Bitless Bridles

Now that so many people in the natural horse world are taking more into consideration with regards to how their horses feel. There has been a steady and fast rise in the amount of riders that choose to use a bitless bridle on their horse. There are several variations of these and when used correctly can bring more comfort to the horse, that is best suited to one. This has pleased many Equine Therapists (as well as horses!) as it shows that those owners, by investigating these options, are thinking of their horses welfare and comfort. Of course it is not to say that many horses aren't comfortable in their bits and can continue with them. Having a bit in the horses mouth can, for some riders bring a sense of security thinking that this means they will be able to stop their horse should it bolt. This is a myth as in, in truth no horse can be stopped using a bit. If anything many will try to run further still, by the pain being inflicted by the trying to make them stop using their mouths. The difference between a bit and bitless bridle could be held in comparison to a collar or a harness on a dog. Which do you feel if the more respectful?

Types of bitless bridles available

The Rope Hackamore: This bitless bridle is very similar to a rope halter. Except that it has more room at the bottom to tie the rope reins.

The English Hackamore - This bitless bridle has a strap that goes across the nose to which metal shanks are fixed and the reins attached. If pressure is used them it will cause leverage pressure across the horses nose and poll. Some riders consider this a more harsh form of bitless bridle. Though the harshness of any bridle could be viewed as, having more to do with the hands that hold the reins, rather than the actual make up of the bridle.

The Dr Cook - There are various copies of this bridle available as well as the branded Dr Cook model. This is a bridle that has cross over straps under the jaw so if the reins are used the pressure it gives will be distributed around the whole head. This includes, the nose, the poll and the sides of the face.

The Scawbrig - This bitless bridle is very similar to a plain head collar except that the part that goes over the nose isn't fixed under the chin. Instead it has a ring each side as it passes through the side cheek pieces of the bridle. This allows the reins to be attached. The pressure comes through using the reins, causing the nose band to tighten.

The Side Pull - This bitless bridle is the kindest of all of the bridles. It is basically a head collar with a brow band and throat lash.

The Matrix Bitless Bridle.

This bridle converts to all the different types of bitless bridle.

Available from www.bitlessandbarefoot.com

The Centaur Experience

This is the name that I have given for when the horse and riders energies combine. This enables the rider and the horse to ride as 'one'. Through connecting with the horses energies they are able to hear our thoughts, and they ours.

In order to try this, the horse must be a safe one that is used to being ridden bareback and must stand quietly first when asked. This involves the horse needing to be grounded through the earth star first.

The rider should then sit on their horse bareback. (This enables there to be no restriction between horse and rider). The horse should be wearing a head collar with reins. The rider should close their eyes and take a few deep breaths, whilst offering the intention for their horse to connect with them. For most people this will either come as an energy type feeling or just a knowing that they are connected. Once this has been established the rider then needs to bring energy up through their right or their left arm, as if it were the horse's leg. As they are connect to the horse, emotionally, physically and spiritually. As this is done slowly there should first be a shift in the horses leg as the request is felt and then slowly but deliberately the horse will start to walk off on its correct leg. Once this has happened ask the horse to stop again using your energy by 'earthing' it through your spinal column and into the horse. Once this has been done, thank your horse for its wonderful response. Now try again with the other leg.

This I believe is what true riding is about, the firm and energetic connection between horse and rider. Once this connection is made there leaves no room for doubt that you have indeed experienced the true unity between the horse and yourself.

Whilst you are doing this also be aware of anything that you physically feel. As the energy comes up through your arm, does it 'stick' anywhere? This could imply an energy blockage in the horse's leg somewhere or the shoulder. Or do you feel any ache or stiffness as in your own arm as the horse begins to move?. If you do this may indicate a physical discomfort in the horse.

If you do not have access to a horse to do this exercise, or one that you feel is suitable. Think of a horse you know and do the exercise through visualisation in your mind. By doing it this way you should still be able to see and feel the desired responses.

The Horse as a Guide

It is often the case when we work with and have a special friendship with horses that some will become our guides. This part of the horse has elected to work with us through it's higher connections to the universe. They pass on information that will not only help us in our lives, but also in our work with other horses. These horses may come in the form of your own horse, one you have lost in the past, or could even be a client's horse. When these horses choose to connect with us they can give us valuable insights as to how to conduct healing sessions, not only on themselves but on other horses that we work with. Not only this, but they are also able to pass on information about the emotional states of the horse and its past lives as well. Also anything we may have missed ourselves which is important with regards to the horse or healing that it needs. This is a very natural process that can either take place in our woken state or our dream time. These horses have chosen to work with us and are there for us to connect to when needed. This is a wonderful gift to us that they offer. So when working with horses in this way, always be sure to thank them and to ask them if there is anything that they need from us by way of balance.

It is not unusual for a horse that has taken on this type of role or has the stellar gateway chakra open. To be able to read their owner and other people that they come into contact with uncanny accuracy. This may even be knowledge that they have about that person's health or emotional state before they even met them. When we open our self up to horses that are able to share their insights with us they see everything to do with us, down to every single thought.

Exercise

Try closing your eyes and taking a few deep breaths. Then ask to be shown your horse guide and any message that they need you to hear. The image may not be clear, it may come as a feeling instead. What do you feel? What is their message for you?

Sympathy vs. Empathy

Some people can often confuse sympathy and empathy. Though they are connected and similar, they are actually on reflection quite different as well. This is because depending on which we choose to work with. The feeling that we get and the way in which we then view and feel about the horse, can change considerably.

Sympathy is the ability to feel for the horse with the horse. By working with sympathy we can allow our self to be dragged into their own personal drama. We then take this information home with us and it can play on our emotional state. When this happens we can find it hard to keep a professional distance and balanced view over just what is going on. The ego may also be considered to play a part in this. On the other hand, when we work with empathy, we can identify with and understand the horse's emotional state. We are still able to step back and keep a professional distance. Whilst totally understanding just how deeply the trauma goes for the horse. It enables us then to work in a way that is still for their highest good, with a full understanding of what needs to be done and how to do it. Whilst at the same time not becoming emotionally involved and therefore, biased to any one outcome.

In simple terms empathy is strength, sympathy is weakness. So when working with any kind of healing our feelings towards our client (in this case the horse), should undoubtedly be one of empathy not sympathy. We don't want to take the horse's worries on ourselves and take them home with us. As this can affect our work with the future horses that need us.

Negative Emotions

A horse can carry negative emotions that may cause it to kick, strike out, bite and become generally frustrated and angry. By the time this has finished playing out. They have exhausted their negative emotional energy so are no longer suppressing it.

The problem being that whilst the above is all well and good, it also has negative outcomes such as putting the horse, other horses nearby or people around the horse in danger. The behaviour that comes from repressed emotion doesn't have to be there in the first place. Ultimately there is no actual reason for the horse to have to repress these emotions, when in a correct environment with the right person. Sadly many horses are passed on from bad homes and bad owners, bringing with them enormous negative suppressed emotions that need an outlet.

It may well be that in the horse's last home or even homes before that the owner, other people and horses it was around wouldn't allow the horse to express itself. In a way that it felt it needed to, or even that the horse didn't know how to express itself full stop. Even when given the opportunity. Just because the horse may choose to deny the existence of the emotion by ignoring it and suppressing it, it doesn't mean it will go away. Each of these emotions will carry their own unique energy frequency many of which will be 'housed' in a particular organ of the physical body. Once the negative emotion has found somewhere in the body to 'live'. It will make itself at home causing emotional disruption by way of an energetic distorted frequency.

The Organs and their Associated Emotions

The Lungs – Grief and sadness

The Liver – Anger and resentment

The Large Intestine – Stuck and rigid emotions

The Small Intestine – Rejection, shock and feelings of abandonment

The Kidneys – Fear

The Gall Bladder – Resentment and depression

The Thyroid/Adrenal – Confusion and paranoia

The Spleen/Pancreas – Worry and low self-esteem

The Stomach – Disgust and despair

The Heart – Sadness and shock

The Bladder – Timidity

Once these disruptions have already developed in the horse's energy field, it is logical that the horse's emotional and physical responses will change accordingly. In time if these disruptions are not sorted out and the emotional state of the horse goes unattended, the horse's body will begin to suffer and its emotional state may deteriorate.

Once we remove these limiting energetic disruptions we then need to 'restock' the horse's meridian system with a positive energy to replace the negative.

Bach Flower Remedies

There are now a large number of companies producing different kinds of flower remedies. The most commonly known of and used in the UK are the Bach Flower Remedies. Throughout the world flower remedies have been made and used for many decades. They work by helping to balance the emotions of the person or the animal that is taking them.

They are very easy to make and as they are preserved traditionally in brandy, they also have a very long shelf life. You may like to refer the internet and search for how you can make your own. Bach Flower Remedies are a combination of thirty-eight plant and flower based remedies, each one specially devised to treat a different feeling or emotion. They can help you to manage the emotional demands of everyday life. The original flower remedies are made according to the exact traditions of Dr. Edward Bach in the 1930's.

The Bach Flower Remedies work by stimulating the body's own capacity to heal itself. By balancing negative feelings and emotions, helping you to take control of your life and enabling you to feel good about yourself. The Bach Flower Remedies are unique, they are simple to use, are suitable for your horses and yourself and are widely available from all major pharmacies and health food stores.

Bach Flower History

A doctor named Edward Bach created the Bach Flower Remedies. He was working in Harley Street in the 1930's. 'A healthy mind is a healthy body' was his philosophy, he was very much ahead of his time. Back in the 1930's the link between emotional and physical health was little if at all acknowledged. Unlike today where psychosomatic illness is well known of and documented.

Dr. Bach devised a system of seven major emotional groups under which people could be classified. These included: Fear, uncertainty and loneliness. He categorised thirty-eight negative states of mind under these groups. Then using his knowledge of homoeopathy, Dr. Bach formulated a plant or flower based remedy to treat each of these emotional states. These are the unique Bach Flower Remedies that we are still using to this day.

The Dr. Edward Bach Centre, Mount Vernon, Oxfordshire is where Dr. Bach lived and worked., discovering his healing flowers in the natural surrounding fields and hedgerows. These same flower locations are still used in the preparation of the Bach Flower Remedies by the present makers. Who continue the tradition and dedication to maintaining the method and use of the remedies as intended. The Centre also acts as the education and training base for the Bach Flower Remedies.

There are varying ideas on how repeatedly giving an incorrect flower remedy affects the horse. Many people feel that it causes no harm. However, it can also be argued that if something has the ability to work at restoring balance when needed. Then it also has the ability to cause disharmony when taken and not needed, in much the same way as we understand homeopathy to work.

Here are the 38 remedies, and their commonly known indications.

Agrimony Putting on a brave face. The concealing of fear. Hurt or inadequacy behind a cheerful face.

Aspen Fear of the unknown origin or without an obvious cause. Feelings of being overwhelmed by emotions or images that arise out of the blue.

Beech Arrogance. Narrow mindedness, hypercritical and intolerance of others.

Centaury Easily led or manipulated by others. Good-natured but weak willed, easily exploited. Self sacrificing.

Cerato Lack of confidence or uncertainty in own judgment. Indecisive and wanting approval and reassurance from others. The self-doubter.

Cherry Plum Fear of loosing control. Mind filled with unfounded or irrational thoughts or emotions. Erratic state.

Chestnut Bud Repeating the same mistakes. Unable to learn the lesson from previous experience. Caught in a vicious cycle of repetition.

Chicory A possessive and demanding attitude. Expecting too much from others. All take and no give. The martyr. Lack of inner fulfillment. Jealousy based on selfishness.

Clematis Absentminded and inattentive. Ungrounded or dreamy state. Living in a fantasy.

Crab Apple Self-disgust. Over reaction to minor imperfection. A loss of perspective, distracted by fine details.

Elm Overwhelmed by responsibility. Unable to make even a simple decision. Feeling inadequate and overwhelmed or exhausted by a task or request.

Gentian Depression of a known origin. Easily discouraged. Despondent and sceptical. The eternal pessimist.

Gorse Despair and hopelessness. 'What's the use' attitude. The pessimist. Giving up even on a chance for survival.

Heather Self-centred but not self-pitying. Desperate for an audience. The needy child. Possessiveness.

Holly Envy or hatred. Malicious feelings. Jealousy and resentment. Being hard-hearted, with a general display of ungenerousness.

Honeysuckle Living in the past. Missing the good old days and not living in the present. Unfulfilled dreams.

Hornbeam Apathy. Insufficiently challenged mentally. Exhausted from mundane routine. Headache or exhaustion from over thinking.

Impatiens Impatience. Frustration that things aren't happening quickly enough. Irritability Doesn't suffer fools gladly.

Larch Lack of confidence. Inferiority complex. Overcautious and so overly constrained that they will not try anything for fear of failure. Feeling useless. Weak-willed.

Mimulus Fear of known reason. Burdened by many different fears. Reserved and sensitive. Shy and timid. Fear about certain things. Passive.

Mustard Dark depression. A black cloud depression with lethargy and lack of drive. Depression that arises without obvious cause. Hopelessness.

Oak Exhaustion from overwork and over thinking. Struggling bravely against adversity. Pacifist type personalities.

Olive Exhaustion. Extreme fatigue and sick with exhaustion. Physical and mental tiredness.

Pine Guilt complex. Putting oneself down. Blames oneself for underachievement and takes on blame for others. Despondent.

Red Chestnut Altruism, self sacrifice. Overly concerned for others. Unable to let go. Suffering, or overly feeling fear for love ones.

Rock Rose Acute fear and panic, Panic attacks. Sudden alert state. Paralysed with fear. Anxiety with increased heart rate.

Rock Water Self-denial. Imposing strict or rigid rules on themselves. Ignoring inner needs. Being unaware of how hard they are on themselves.

Scleranthus Mood swings. Indecisive, opinions and moods change from one moment to the next. Erratic thought or behaviours.

Star of Bethlehem Trauma - both mental and physical. The after affects of physical or emotional shock. Grief and bereavement.

Sweet Chestnut Despair. Acute anxiety and anguish brought about through shock. Acute desperation. Feeling weak and vulnerable, or can't cope.

Vervain Over-enthusiastic in ones conduct. Fanatical or highly-strung. Obsessive on ones approach.

Vine Domineering. Applies pressure to others to achieve their goals. Inflexible. Over confident and bullying. Inconsiderate and lacking compassion for others.

Walnut Major life changes. New challenges. Coping with difficult transitional periods. Feelings of vulnerability due to change.

Water Violet Proud, reserved and detached. Appearing superior to others, yet emotionally detached. Craves or enjoys silence.

White Chestnut Overwhelmed by persistent thoughts going round and round in their head. Prisoner to one's thoughts. Trouble sleeping.

Wild Oat Lack of commitment to a path. Opportunities present yet still feel unfulfilled. No certain path in their life.

Wild Rose Apathy and lack of interest in life. Lack of ambition. Sense of resignation. Dispassionate.

Willow Resentful. 'Poor me'. Hard done by and feels like one of lifes victims. Passive resentment. Negative feelings that turn inwards. Self-pitying.

Rescue Remedy

This remedy is widely known of and used for cases sudden trauma and extreme fear amongst other uses. It is made up of the following remedies combined: Impatiens, Star of Bethlehem, Cherry Plum, Rock Rose, Clematis.

Flower Remedy Dosage

The standard dosage for a horse would be 10 drops each of one or more remedies in a days worth of drinking water. This way the horse is taking the remedy at intervals throughout the day and night. For more extreme cases the remedy can be given straight into the mouth making sure that it touches the soft tissues. Please be aware that these remedies usually come in bottles with glass droppers, so caution is advised (alternatively you can add a few drops to a piece of wet food so that it is still able to touch the soft tissues of the mouth). If you are in any doubt as to which remedies to use it may be advisable to contact a Bach Flower Remedy Practitioner who is qualified at more depth.

Resources

Holly Davis
Animal Communicator and Therapist
www.hollydavis.co.uk

Elenore Bowden-Bird
Aulanda Park Liberty
www.apequineliberty.com.au

Graeme Green
Horse Healing and Land Healing
www.themindfulhorse.wordpress.com

Susan Duckworth
Hoofboots, Bitless Bridles, Neem and much more.
www.bitlessandbarefoot.com

Alan Howell
Medical Grade Essential Oils and Powders
www.shechina.co.uk

Thunderbrook
Organic and Natural Horse Feeds and Educational Articles
www.thunderbrook.co.uk

Terry Shubrook
Kinesiology and Healing
www.terryshubrook.co.uk

The Masterson Method
www.mastersonmethod.com

Victoria Standen
Zoopharmocognosy / Animal Aromatics
www.harmonyhealingforanimals.co.uk

Liz Harris
McTimoney, Massage, Reiki
www.lizharris.co.uk

Suzanna Thomas
Centre for workshops and holistic horse care and products
www.spiritofthenaturalhorse.com

Henry Cumming
Horse Healing and Whispering
www.henrycumming.com

Kirsty Cooper
Horse Hair Jewellery
www.finedesignequinegifts.co.uk

Teresa Perrin
Bowen Therapy
www.teresaperrin.co.uk

Kay Emmerson
Sports Massage, Equine Aromatics, Kinesiology
www.equine-therapeutics.co.uk

Dawn Cox
Horse Rhythm Beads
www.angelhorse.co.uk

Helen Jacks - Hewett
McTimoney, Sports Massage
www.horse-back.co.uk

Rosie Hume
Masterson Method
Norfolk and North Suffolk
Tel: 07786 545977
Email: rosie3319@gmail.com

Lou Wilks
Masterson Method
www.naturallyhorse.co.uk

Julie Dexter
EMRT Bowen and Crystal Healing
www.bowenbalancing.co.uk

Emma Knowles
Veterinary Physiotherapy and Equine Touch
emma4et@hotmail.com
07921258752

www.theequinetouch.com

www.navp.co.uk

ABOUT THE AUTHOR

Holly has been working as a profession Animal Communicator and Therapist since 1999. She currently lives in Wales with her seven cats and three Arabian horses.

She is the Author of several books and courses on animal therapies. These are available throughout the UK as well as Internationally.

She has a keen interest in natural behaviour and medicine as well as, psychological disorders in animals. A huge amount of her time is spent helping people to understand their animals. Aid in their recovery and create a better life for them.

Holly was one of the first Animal Communicators to teach workshops in England and is the Author of the first recognised Animal Communication Diploma in the UK.

Her accredited courses are available through Stonebridge College, links for which can be found on her website.

For information about Holly's other books, please visit

www.hollydavis.co.uk

Sometimes horse whispers....

Sometimes horse screams.....

Just how, if and when horses are healed and heard.

Is down to each and every one of us, as guardians of the magnificent horses and animal kingdom.

Be the one that helps to create change.

You may not be able to change the whole world, but you can change the world for at least one horse.